KOHELES

MAN'S QUEST *for* HAPPINESS

and its

INEXTRICABLE TIE

with the

INESCAPABLE FRUSTRATIONS *of* AMBITION

Rabbi Israel Chait
STUDENT'S NOTES FROM LECTURES

YESHIVA B'NEI TORAH
www.YBT.org

1st EDITION

CONTENTS

Part IV: Themes of Koheles

Student's Words

INTRODUCTION

"Koheles: Man's Quest for Happiness" are student's notes from Rabbi Israel Chait's lectures on King Solomon's book covering metaphysics[1], philosophy, psychology, morality and Torah.

In the early 1970s, Rabbi Chait presented a thorough and insightful analysis of Koheles' first chapter, comprising Part I of this book. In 1986 and 1987 Rabbi Chait gave a series of lectures covering many of Koheles' remaining chapters, comprising Parts II, III and IV. Not all verses were addressed, therefore there are gaps in the sequence of verses.

Rabbi Chait deciphers King Solomon's expressions, lessons, metaphors and surface contradictions. He enlightens us to the myriad of conscious fantasies, the unconscious, frustrations, conflicts, values, ambitions and attitudes confronting man in his quest for a fulfilling life.

Using himself as the subject, King Solomon experimented with all possible lifestyles, from indulging in riches and drink, to lives of frivolity and sophistication. At every turn, the king records his reactions and exposes the fallacies behind blind ambitions and ideals. With his keen wisdom, King Solomon unveiled the many recesses of man's psychological dynam-

---

1) Metaphysics (*meta* is Greek for higher or beyond) refers to a branch of philosophy dealing with matters higher than the physical world. These matters include God (including His justice, kindness, His role as Creator and other "traits"), angels, wisdom, concepts, knowledge, man's soul, and natural laws. These matters are not physical nor exist within the physical world. Thus, they are termed metaphysical matters: matters higher than the physical.

ics, hidden from most people. What are man's assumptions regarding happiness? What are man's psychological faculties, dynamics and their pitfalls? How does man fool himself into chasing fantasies and unattainable goals? Why do he think certain objectives and actions will provide happiness, and why must they fail? And what role does the fantasy of immortality play in human ambition? Koheles is a thorough and honest analysis of these matters, and more.

To gain the most from Koheles, we must appreciate that God granted unparalleled wisdom to King Solomon at age 12 when his father King David died and King Solomon ascended the throne. God appeared to him in a prophetic dream saying, *"Ask what I shall give you."* [2] Solomon responded, *"Give to your servant a hearing heart to judge your people between good and evil..."*[3] God granted this to him, saying, *"...as you have requested this matter, and you did not ask for long days, and you did not request riches, and you did not ask for the death of your enemies, and you requested understanding to hear judgement...behold, I do as your words; behold I give to you a heart that is wise and understanding, that like you, there was no one before, and after you, there will not arise anyone like you."*[4] Leaders from all nations came to hear King Solomon's wisdom[5] and were astonished at his insights.

The reader will be amazed at King Solomon's genius. As

---

2) Kings I, 3:5
3) Kings I, 3:9
4) Kings I, 3:11,12
5) Kings I, 5:14

a prophet gifted with Divine knowledge earning the Rabbis' praise as the wisest man ever next to Moses[6], we are offered the singular opportunity of joining King Solomon in witnessing God's wisdom. The king desired to share his wisdom with all others, to help us all understand which life path and choices will secure true happiness, and avoid grief and misfortune. But as he wrote in metaphor and in apparent contradictions[7], his words require the greatest attention and sensitivity.

In Part 1, the 1970s Lectures, Rabbi Chait's analysis of Koheles' first chapter reveals King Solomon's depth of human understanding. This includes explanations of otherwise cryptic metaphors with unique and marvelous insights into the primary components and workings of man's psyche. Perhaps it is no coincidence that in both Genesis' and Koheles' opening chapters, we find discussions of immortality, sin, fantasy[8], the instincts, desire, rivers, blame, remorse, and other psychological parallels as prerequisite study for understanding man and how to achieve happiness.

Rabbi Chait's lectures on Koheles offer us a unique and valuable opportunity to learn how to guide our lives not only as followers of Torah, but as human beings.

Note: All footnotes are student's words.

---

6) *Guide for the Perplexed*, book III, chap. LIV
7) This was done to keep wisdom hidden among the wise men, *chachamim*.
8) The snake enticed Eve to eat the forbidden fruit. We then read, *"The woman (Eve) saw the fruit was good to eat...(Gen. 3:5,6)."* Eve's "seeing" refers to her fantasy about the fruit's potential benefits.

Part I: The Psyche and Man's Quest
WHO WAS KING SOLOMON?

דִּבְרֵי קֹהֶלֶת בֶּן־דָּוִד מֶלֶךְ בִּירוּשָׁלָ͏ם

*"The words of Koheles, the son of David, king in Jeru-
salem (1:1)."*

What is the meaning of *"Koheles?"* Why did King Solomon
identify himself as the *"son of David"* and as *"king?"* Why is it
crucial that we know that he reigned *"in Jerusalem?"*

The name of a wise author prods the reader to ap-
ply extensive thought. For if one were to pick up a
book written by a writer of average caliber, he would
not carefully analyze the ideas, if there were any.

But if one were about to read a book authored by Albert Einstein, he would certainly approach such a book with the care required to fully grasp and understand Einstein's message. An intellect as great as Einstein certainly wrote matters of great worth. Therefore, King Solomon identified himself in order to alert the reader that his teachings cannot simply be read, but require careful thought.

Koheles means "to gather," as in *kehila,* a gathering of congregants. Applied to King Solomon, the "gathering" to which he referred was his wisdom, which the king possessed in abundance. The King wished to share with his readers that since Koheles is a work on metaphysics, which requires knowledge from all areas, "Koheles" conveys this idea. In other words, the King wished to say, *"I gathered much knowledge and therefore I have authority to write this book."* King Solomon also wrote Proverbs. But as Proverbs addresses ethics alone, the only knowledge required is ethical knowledge.

Another explanation why the name Koheles was used is due to the fact that King Solomon always spoke in large gatherings comprised of wise men, the *Chochmei Yisrael.* But we must ask why the king was concerned to share that he spoke to large groups of wise men. The reason is that King Solomon's conclusions benefited from other wise men, to whom he was able to subject his thoughts to their scrutiny. A person who learns by himself tends to think that his ideas are correct. Having contrasted his ideas with men of wisdom, King Solomon eliminated personal error. The reason for stating Koheles here and not in Proverbs, is because Proverbs is relatively simple; it was not that necessary to tell us that he studied with others.

Why *"son of David?"* Since one's teacher impacts his knowledge, King Solomon shared that his teacher was his father, King David. Again, to urge the reader to pay careful attention to the lessons of Koheles, the king reiterated that he was trained by one of the greatest minds.

King Solomon also states he was *"king in Jerusalem."* This was to convey that he lived in a rich environment, which also contributes to one's knowledge. As king of Jerusalem, he was the one person in the choice societal role to take full advantage of all which that environment offered.

Why in Proverbs does King Solomon refer to himself as *"king of Israel?"* Proverbs addresses ethical matters, which is knowledge pertaining to people. Therefore, he uses the term Israel to indicate the nation. Meaning, he is intelligent politically; he knows how to relate to the people of Israel.

KOHELES

FANTASY & REALITY

הֶבֶל הֲבָלִים אָמַר קֹהֶלֶת הֲבֵל הֲבָלִים
הַכֹּל הָבֶל

*"Futility of futilities, said Koheles, futility of futilities;
all is futile (1:2)."*

As this verse mentions the term futile seven times[1], the Rabbis teach it references the seven days of Creation. What do the Rabbis' mean? This means to say that King Solomon identified the physical world alone as futile, explaining why he repeated *"futile"* seven times. The universe – not the metaphysical world

---

1) "Futile" in the singular is mentioned three times, and twice in the plural (meaning at least two) totaling 7 mentions, correlating to the seven days of Creation.

13

– was created during the seven days. The physical alone is futile.

The Written Law, *Torah she'bicsav,* contains allusions to the Oral Law, *Torah she'baal peh.* But the Rabbis didn't figure out from the Written Law, what the Oral Law is. The Oral Law too was received at Sinai and transmitted, as was the Written Law. The Rabbis knew the Written Law alludes to that which was already known through the Oral Law. Here, the Rabbis did not merely deduce from Koheles that the physical world is futile. They knew this from a careful analysis of the king's works. The Sages are merely using King Solomon's seven mentions of *"futile"* as an allusion to an idea already known.

What is meant by the word *"futile?"* And what is meant by the additional word *"all"* in the phrase, *"all is futile?"* This indicates that more than the physical world is futile. What is that additional thing? Furthermore, why did King Solomon need to write *"said Koheles?"* He already identified himself in the first verse. And a powerful question is, how could King Solomon say that physical creation is futile, while God called creation "good?"[2]

To answer this, we must make a crucial distinction. King Solomon meant that the physical universe is futile, but only when used as an ends. In contrast, God said that it is good when utilized as a means for man to perfect his soul. To be

---

2) Many times in Genesis (chap. 1) God says Creation was "good."

clear, King Solomon identifies creation as futile, only when it is sought for itself as an ends, such as eating for pleasure alone, and not as a means to strengthen one's self to follow God's Torah. God called creation *"good"* inasmuch as man harnesses the physical world to perfect his soul.

King Solomon's repetition of *"futile"* was not to allude to the seven days of Creation. That, as we said, was known from the Tradition, the *Mesora*. Just as the Torah repeats topics many times with the objective of emphasis (viz., the Love of God, the Exodus, idolatry, etc.), so too, the king's repetition was for emphasis. However, wherein lies the importance in his second sentence? What precisely is he emphasizing? Just as the Torah repeats only those matters that are foundations to Judaism, King Solomon too must be repeating only that which he feels is crucial. What is it?

Additionally, the reason why the king states *"said Koheles"* is because he is again stressing how important this idea is. This first statement is so important, that without knowing its meaning, you can't go any further in this work. Therefore, we must understand the meaning of *"futility of futilities."* What kind of formulation is this? King Solomon is describing the phenomenon of fantasy.[3] These are the *"futility of futilities."* One fu-

---

3) An example will illustrate this point. A man will open a magazine and see an advertised new sports car. The red metallic shine, the advertised acceleration speed, and the luxurious leather interior all contribute to the creation of something other than the car...what we term the "fantasy." This fantasy is the imagined happiness one fabricates he will experience with his new acquisition...a failed attempt to secure happiness.

tility is seeking the physical world as an ends. The second is the fantasy man creates connected to that desire. But how do fantasies work? How do they fool us to believe that if we possessed or experienced "X", we would be happy forever? What provides this conviction?

There are two factors: 1) the quality of the fantasy, i.e., the new car, and 2) the quantity of time we will enjoy the car. This quantity is somehow left out of the picture. That's why one feels that the enjoyment will never cease. But it does cease and that's when you create a new fantasy. A person projects the imagined enjoyment into the future, indefinitely. So the conviction of pure pleasure and no pain emanates from the false notion that enjoyments are endless. And since one feels that the imagined pleasure will not end, he chases the fantasy. In his *Guide for the Perplexed*, Maimonides teaches that in order to have pleasure, one must have 1) the desired object, and 2) novelty. If there is no novelty, there won't be pleasure. So when one fantasizes, he projects his initial relationship of novelty into the future. He assumes the feeling of newness will endure without end. In a fantasy, the initial excitement that always fades in reality, is not recognized. However, fantasy cannot satisfy as reality. For if it did, one wouldn't need reality. The fantasy would be as good as reality.

"Futility of futilities" means there exists a twofold emptiness. One emptiness is reality: the car cannot provide indefinite happiness. The other emptiness is the fantasy which is created out of the real life. The emptinesses are 1) the physical as an ends, and 2) the imagination or fantasy of that assumed pleasure. The one phenomenon which diminishes the fantasy is mortality. When one realizes that his life is going to end, his fantasies end as well. This applies to those of old age or subjected to terminal disease. The reality of death causes the imagination to cease because it cuts short the backdrop essential for projecting *endless* fantasy.

"Futility of futilities" requires one to abandon fantasy life. Koheles is an attempt to go beyond the fantasies, to see life as it really is. Additionally, fantasy does not exist regarding spiritual matters. That's why *"futility of futilities"* applies to the physical alone.

ACCOMPLISHMENT & BENEFIT

מַה־יִּתְרוֹן לָאָדָם בְּכָל־עֲמָלוֹ שֶׁיַּעֲמֹל
תַּחַת הַשָּׁמֶשׁ

*"What addition is there to man in all his labor at which
he labors under the sun (1:3)?"*

There exists only reality. In contrast, fantasy is non-existent.
There are no *"additions"* (benefits) to man's imaginations. For
example, man imagines he benefits from leaving over an em-
pire to his children, or he fantasizes of the prestige from a high
office. However, these are all empty and there is no benefit to

them; only a fantasy. What is real, is man's labor[4]. What is unreal is the imagined legacy, or how man thinks others view him as he attains a higher office.

What is meant by *"under the sun"?* This refers to the physical world: that which is literally under the sun. As we stated, if used as an end and not as a means to study God, Torah and creation to arrive at a love of God and to perfect ourselves, the physical world is futile. Therefore, King Solomon states that the physical world is futile.

Rashi says the word *"under"* (tachas) means "instead." Meaning, there is no benefit for that which is under the sun, i.e., the physical world as an end. But that which is not under the sun, – metaphysical pursuits – there is a benefit. The metaphysical is that which is "instead of the sun" (instead of the physical).

Therefore, the verse should be read as follows: What benefit is there under the sun? None. But that which is instead of the sun, does in fact provide benefit.

---

4) Man provides for himself through labor. But the imagined satisfaction of leaving an inheritance is diminished by the worry if it reaches his children, or if they will use it wisely. And the prestige of high office exists only in the imagination: it is not real. That is, the identical labor performed by an official, is performed by blue-collar workers. This work is reality, but the official's reality does not differ from the lower-class worker. When the official is in front of cameras or sees himself in newspapers, he then imagines a sense of prestige. But this feeling fades when he is off-camera and not in the spotlight. He then strives to make headlines once again. It is a vicious cycle met with frustration more than with honor.

IMMORTALITY

דּוֹר הֹלֵךְ וְדוֹר בָּא וְהָאָרֶץ לְעוֹלָם עֹמָדֶת

"One generation passes, and another generation comes;
but the Earth abides for ever (1:4)."

The Rabbis teach, *"A person does not die with half of his de-*
sires in hand. For he who has a hundred, desires to make of it two
hundred."[5] This means that the fantasy exceeds reality. King
Solomon addresses one of the two fantasies that drive people.
One fantasy is regarding objects or possessions. The second
fantasy deals with man's feeling of permanence. Man's fanta-

---

5) Koheles Rabbah, 1:13

sies make sense, but only if he's going to live forever. An idea has two parts: 1) the idea itself, and 2) the emotional effect of the idea. Every person knows the idea that he or she will die. But the emotional effect is usually denied. This enables man to believe his fantasy is achievable. It is impossible to live without the fantasy of immortality. It expresses itself one way or another.

The meaning behind this verse is that the average person looks at life as the only reality. He cannot perceive himself as a single speck in a chain of billions of people and events, where he plays but a minuscule role, and passes on. Any feeling man has of greatness comes from the feeling of immortality. Immortality never reaches into lusts; only ego.

Here, the king places the correct perspective before us. We look at the world as starting with our birth, and as dying with our death. Our previous verse dealt with the fantasy of pleasures. This verse deals with the fantasy of immortality. But there is also a connection between the two fantasies. As soon as one sees that his life is nearing its end, he cannot enjoy things anymore. The enjoyment of things is tied to the belief of an endless lifetime in which to enjoy them.

Man's attention is directed primarily toward his well-being. If a life-threatening situation faces man, this is the most devastating experience; everything else doesn't make that much difference to him. Once a person faces death, all fantasies of pleasures don't carry much weight.

Rashi says on this verse, *"Who are those that exist forever? They are the humble ones that bow down to the ground."* Rashi means there is in fact an eternity: this is for righteous people – *tzaddikim* – expressed as those who humble themselves, *"bowing to the ground."* The soul of the Tzaddik will endure forever.

KOHELES

LUSTS

וְזָרַח הַשֶּׁמֶשׁ וּבָא הַשָּׁמֶשׁ וְאֶל־מְקוֹמוֹ
שׁוֹאֵף זוֹרֵחַ הוּא שָׁם

*"The sun also rises, and the sun sets, and hastens to its
place where it rises again (1:5)."*

King Solomon continues his illustration of man's psyche,
now engaging metaphor. This metaphor of the sun describes
man's search for *taiva*, lusts. Man obtains the object of his desires, *"the sun rises."* But then the experience passes, *"the sun
sets."* Man then chases the desire again, *"and hastens to its place
where it rises again."*

PROGRESS

הוֹלֵךְ אֶל־דָּרוֹם וְסוֹבֵב אֶל־צָפוֹן סוֹבֵב סֹבֵב
הוֹלֵךְ הָרוּחַ וְעַל־סְבִיבֹתָיו שָׁב הָרוּחַ

*"[The wind] goes toward the south, and circles around
towards the north; encircling, encircling the wind trav-
els and on its circuits the wind returns (1:6)."*

The king is not teaching patterns of weather. This work is
about man's quest for happiness. Therefore, this verse must
be considered in that light. Here, the king addresses the perspective of the evil man, the *Rasha* (wind is a metaphor for the
Rasha). The Rasha feels as though he's succeeding, or going

places in life, viz., north, south, etc. But in reality, he goes nowhere: *"and the wind returns again according to its circuits."* The wind repeats the same path.

Verse 1:5 deals with how reality operates: man chases a desire, the experience or brief satisfaction expires, and he repeats his chase. While verse 1:6 deals with the subjective perspective of the Rasha; he attributes a value to his actions, as if "going places." But why is the word *"encircling"* – סֹבֵב – repeated?

The first instance of סוֹבֵב refers to the man's error in following his emotions in the first place. The second סָבַב refers to the fact that man continues on his foolish path. Why does this occur? The first סוֹבֵב (man's error) is committed due to man's lack of reason. The second סָבַב refers to the error in not heeding experience, which should teach man that he was initially in error.[6]

6) Man's failed attempts at obtaining happiness by chasing his lusts are ignored. For we see man repeating fruitless behaviors time and again. This is the second סָבַב, or error where man repeats his error as if "going in circles" as the saying goes.

PSYCHOLOGICAL ENERGY

כָּל־הַנְּחָלִים הֹלְכִים אֶל־הַיָּם וְהַיָּם אֵינֶנּוּ מָלֵא
אֶל־מְקוֹם שֶׁהַנְּחָלִים הֹלְכִים
שָׁם הֵם שָׁבִים לָלָכֶת

*"All the rivers flow to the sea; but the sea is not full;
towards the place where the rivers flow, there they return again to flow (1:7)."*

Verse 1:5 teaches the cycle that man takes with his emotions.
Verse 1:6 tells us that this cycle cannot operate without a bit
of reality: that man feels he is getting somewhere, i.e., north,
south. However, this is a delusion. There are two causes for

man following this foolish cycle. One cause is what King Solomon stated in verse 1:6: man thinks he's getting somewhere. But this is only a secondary cause. The primary cause is based on a need. That need is man's great reservoir of psychological energy.

Man's energy is depicted as a river; a relentless force. *"The sea is not full"* means that man's desires are never quenched. Man is never satisfied because his energies (rivers) are great: *"To the place where the rivers flow, there they return again to flow."*[7]

Man's sense of progress is a rationalization. But this drive is not the primary cause for man's actions. Rather, it is man's great amount of energy which is relentless in his search for satisfaction. Psychological energy is the cause which underlies the rationalization: man's intense energy drives him into a situation where he finds himself rationalizing.

This verse is an exact analogy to the workings of the psyche. The rivers flowing to the sea are the emotions flowing to the desired object. *"Yet the sea is not full,"* i.e., man is not satisfied. This is because the desire is only as enjoyable as its novelty. Once novelty fades, so does the desire for the object. This is what is meant by *"there they return again to flow."* Since novelty

---

7) It is noteworthy that Genesis (2:10-14) also discusses rivers. There too, rivers are interspersed in a description of man. It is possible that King Solomon understood those rivers in Genesis to depict man's inner workings, and he follows suit here by using the identical phenomenon of flowing water to describe some element of man. If this is true, then a study of the rivers in Genesis will yield additional insights into man's psychological nature.

fades away, the waters (man's energies) gather to flow towards yet another desired object.

Furthermore, when one fantasizes about a desired object, he must incorporate into his fantasy the illusion that his satisfaction will be endless. As stated, fantasy requires the desired object, and the feeling that the enjoyment will never end.

FRUSTRATION & SATISFACTION

כָּל־הַדְּבָרִים יְגֵעִים לְא־יוּכַל אִישׁ לְדַבֵּר לֹא־
תִשְׂבַּע עַיִן לִרְאוֹת וְלֹא־תִמָּלֵא אֹזֶן מִשְּׁמֹעַ

"All things are wearisome; man cannot utter it; the eye is not satisfied with seeing, nor the ear filled from hearing (1:8)."

Only these two senses – sight and sound – are used because they are the main senses of desire; they arouse lust more than other senses. Weariness is felt since the amount of energy seeking satisfaction is far greater than what reality offers. Man's design is such, that his desire for satisfaction cannot find satisfaction through physical pleasures. The Rabbis state, *"A person does not die with half of his desires in hand. For he who has a hundred, desires to make of it two hundred."*[8] The Rabbis teach that man will never find satisfaction in physical pleasures. The only way man can satisfy his energies, is through intellectual inquiry; through the pursuit of wisdom.

An example will illustrate why the physical world cannot offer the amount of satisfaction needed. While a person is planning a trip, he experiences pent-up energy due to anticipation that doesn't reach satisfaction until the trip. During his planning stages, he is frustrated. If one spent two months of planning, during which time his energies are frustrated and not yet satisfied, and he experiences just two weeks of actual satisfaction, the person was unsatisfied for two months and satisfied for only two weeks. That's not a good trade-off.[9] We would not say that overall, the person was experiencing a satisfying lifestyle.

---

8) Koheles Rabbah, 1:13
9) Due to man's great energies, the need to plan, additionally stress due to anticipation, man's energies remain frustrated for an extended period of time. This sustained frustration is not worth the brief satisfaction. Other pleasures too are short-lived, accompanied by impossible fantasies and hopes for endless satisfaction, which never occur. All pleasures are quite temporary, and when they suddenly pass, man is left dissatisfied with the experience. Wisdom, on the other hand, experiences no delay. One may engage thought, anytime, anywhere. But primarily, wisdom is the only pursuit that engages all of man's energies, resulting in no frustration and complete satisfaction. This experience of studying God's creations and His Torah is how God designed man to achieve happiness. It is impossible that man can satisfy his abundant energies completely in any pursuit other than using his mind.

MODERNITY

מַה־שֶּׁהָיָה הוּא שֶׁיִּהְיֶה וּמַה־שֶּׁנַּעֲשָׂה הוּא
שֶׁיֵּעָשֶׂה וְאֵין כָּל־חָדָשׁ תַּחַת הַשָּׁמֶשׁ

*"That which was, it will be; and that which was performed
will be performed, and there is nothing new under the
sun (1:9)."*

This verse cannot be referring to the physical world. For if
it were, suggesting "whatever is going to happen already happened" would exclude the possibility of a "first thing." For according to this reasoning, it should have already happened! That
is, the suggestion that there cannot possibly be something new,

we thereby discount a first thing, because first things are in fact new. But, as reason dictates, that the universe cannot exist if it never had a beginning, what King Solomon refers to here must be a non-physical topic. In this verse, the king describes the emotion of "modernity" – the desire for newness.

The motivation behind this desire is that man's pride and contentment are derived from viewing his generation as "the" generation. Man wants to feel secure, and does so by viewing prior generations as archaic, outdated, and that we today have more knowledge. "We're at the forefront," man imagines. He finds support in notions like today's clothing being more stylish, cars are most advanced, and people live "modern" lifestyles. We often hear a scornful tone in that saying, "You're old-fashioned." The latest generation views itself as reaching man's potential, while former generations fell short.

The basis for this emotion is that a person can't face the fact of *"Dor holeich v'dor bah; A generation comes and a generation passes (1:4)."* A person does not feel secure thinking that he's only one in billions of people who come and go on this planet. To compensate, man attempts to elevate himself from past generations. He needs to create a new reality to secure his wishes, denying the truth that he too will soon pass, like all other generations, and that the next generation will view him as outdated. Man attempts to placate his fear by fabricating a feeling of modernity: "Our generation is *the* generation," man feels.

King Solomon responds to this illusion by breaking down this emotion of modernity with his words *"...there is nothing new under the sun."*

Rashi cites how Rebbe Eliezer ben Rav Hurkonus found a new idea regarding metaphysics, *Maaseh Merkava*. Rashi means to distinguish the metaphysical from the physical world. Regarding physical enjoyments, when man feels a new enjoyment surpasses the last one, this imagined escalation in satisfaction is only relative to one's last enjoyment. It is also merely a quantitative difference. However, regarding wisdom and metaphysical matters, when one learns a new idea that unifies or explains various areas of study, this is not a quantitative change from a small idea to a large one. Rather, the first idea was enjoyable, for one perceived wisdom and enjoyed the concept independently. Now, when that individual learns a new idea that helps him to see how many ideas are related, he senses greater enjoyment. This is because wisdom is a knowledge of unification of matters. And when a newly learned concept explains many areas, one unifies more things with this idea, and this offers man great pleasure.[10]

We cannot suggest the pleasure derived from wisdom is relative, like one who buys a new car and then his enjoyment

---

10) Imagine a scientist seeking to explain why objects fall when dropped, why the planets continually revolve around the sun, and why larger planets have more intense effects on matter and light, than do smaller planets. Then, the scientist discovers a new thing called "gravity," explaining all three areas of his inquiry. You can readily appreciate the satisfaction he will experience as he unifies all three phenomena with one newly-discovered law.

fades. Such pleasures are relative to the person's mindset, they vary from person to person, and are relative to other competing pleasures, like newer cars.

But wisdom is absolute. It doesn't depend on the individual for its capability to provide enjoyment. Wisdom is new and enjoyable. That is Rashi's message.

Another reason why the verse states the language of *"was"* and *"performed"* is because this emotion of modernity express-es itself in two forms: 1) modernity of objects, and 2) of ac-tions, or accomplishments.

MODERNITY IN ACTION

יֵשׁ דָּבָר שֶׁיֹּאמַר רְאֵה־זֶה חָדָשׁ הוּא כְּבָר הָיָה
לְעֹלָמִים אֲשֶׁר הָיָה מִלְּפָנֵנוּ

"There is a thing that one says, 'See this, it is new,' it already existed in ancient times that preceded us (1:10)."

How does one express himself in combination with his beliefs of modernity? He seeks support from his environment, saying, "Here is a new thing." This is his attempt to substantiate his philosophy of modernity. But King Solomon tells us that in truth, there is nothing that does not have its origins in ancient times.[11]

---

11) Yes, we will certainly find more modern cars, but carriages always existed. We can invent computers, but ancient forms of computation existed such as the abacus. And although fashion changes, clothing was always a means of demonstrating status.
The message is not to seek pleasure or satisfaction by fabricating greater worth via a sense of advancement for one's era.

LEGACY

אֵין זִכְרוֹן לָרִאשֹׁנִים וְגַם לָאַחֲרֹנִים שֶׁיִּהְיוּ
לֹא־יִהְיֶה לָהֶם זִכָּרוֹן עִם שֶׁיִּהְיוּ לָאַחֲרֹנָה

"There is no remembrance to the first generations, and also to the latter ones there will be no remembrance with those who will be at the end (1:11)."

One might think this verse addresses ordinary recorded history. But this cannot be, for we see that there are records of prior generations.

What this verse describes is the way one thinks he's going to be remembered, and that is as one who lived during the genera-

41

tion of modernity. Since people imagine that their generation is experiencing the peak of any society, they feel their remembrance will be great; as one who partook in breakthroughs, having lived during the era.

This, however, falls short of reality just like the emotion of modernity itself. King Solomon says the first generations harbored this feeling of importance, but they were wrong. We too will think it, yet we will not be remembered this way.

So verse 1:9 is the rule set down which breaks the emotion of modernity: *"That which was, it will be; and that which was performed will be performed, and there is nothing new under the sun."*

Verse 1:10 is showing us how the fantasy is expressed, and King Solomon's breakdown: *"See this, it is new. It already existed in ancient times that preceded us."*

And verse 1:11 addresses the delusion of making a mark in history, striving for the last vestige of modernity. That is, a person might think, *"It's true that past generations weren't really modern because they didn't have what it takes...but we hit upon it!"* The breakdown of this misconception is *"and also to the latter ones there will be no remembrance."* This tells us that if you make this assumption, you're really fooling yourself.

MODERNITY: SELF-APPLIED

אֲנִי קֹהֶלֶת הָיִיתִי מֶלֶךְ עַל־יִשְׂרָאֵל בִּירוּשָׁלָם

*"I am Koheles, I was king over Israel in Jerusalem
(1:12)."*

The message here is told through the phrase *"I was"*.
King Solomon tells us that he was king and that he wasn't overcome with the emotion of modernity. He tells us this so we
should heed his words. This verse qualifies him, and he in turn
qualifies his teachings.

PLEASURE UNMASKED

וְנָתַתִּי אֶת־לִבִּי לִדְרוֹשׁ וְלָתוּר בַּחָכְמָה עַל כָּל־
אֲשֶׁר נַעֲשָׂה תַּחַת הַשָּׁמָיִם הוּא | עִנְיַן רָע נָתַן
אֱלֹהִים לִבְנֵי הָאָדָם לַעֲנוֹת בּוֹ

"And I applied my heart to inquire and search with wisdom on all that is performed under the heaven; it is an evil matter God gave to the sons of man to afflict him (1:13)."

If one searches all physical pleasures (*"under the heaven"*) wisdom unveils how dissatisfying[12] these things are. That is

12) Pleasures are dissatisfying when sought as an ends, as King Solomon states herein. But when engaged as part of the Torah lifestyle, in proper measure and at proper times, the physical world does offer pleasure and satisfaction. These are the real pleasures, in contrast

45

one[13] reason it is an evil matter. As King Solomon used his keen intelligence to examine the phenomenon of man engaging assumed pleasures, he exposed the fallacies that typical men delude themselves to view as valuable and pleasurable, bringing about the *affliction* described in this verse.

---

to man's many fantasies that lead to frustration.
13) Another "affliction" is mentioned in the chapter entitled *Investigation*: "Man's task to search out a philosophy is something which is an evil matter because man has no natural means which tell him how to live."

KNOWLEDGE IS PAIN

כִּי בְּרֹב חָכְמָה רָב־כָּעַס
וְיוֹסִיף דַּעַת יוֹסִיף מַכְאוֹב

*"For in much wisdom there is much anger; and he that
increases knowledge, increases sorrow (1:18)."*

When man gains knowledge, he comes to learn the things
which he considered enjoyable, truly provide no pleasure.
Thereby, he loses those enjoyments.

Man possesses many faculties and attitudes, including wishes and his rational element, his intellect. Once man rationally

47

unveils his wishes as empty pursuits, he becomes depressed. For example, the enjoyment of sports is the measuring of perfection of a useless art. Once man sees this enjoyment is truly foolish, he loses that desire. He realizes these "sport abilities" don't serve any real purpose in enjoying life. "Ignorance is bliss." That is, bliss remains until wisdom exposes the pursuit as foolish. Man thereby loses what he felt was pleasurable, resulting in anger and sorrow. Anger is aroused because increased knowledge removes the imagined pleasure, resulting in a desire to change this situation. Anger is the emotional expression of man unsuccessfully attempting to change an intolerable reality.

INTOXICATION

אָמַרְתִּי אֲנִי בְּלִבִּי לְכָה־נָּא אֲנַסְּכָה בְשִׂמְחָה
וּרְאֵה בְטוֹב וְהִנֵּה גַם־הוּא הָבֶל

"And I said in my heart, 'I will go now and gladden myself with wine and experience the good'. And behold, it too is futile (2:1)."

King Solomon realized the imagined pleasures were not enjoyable. His next attempt to find fulfillment was intoxication. His plan was to escape reality by putting himself in a state where the critical faculty[14] would not function. But this too he calls futile. The next verse explains why.

---

14) Man's intellect and conscience impress values on him, which intoxication weakens, causing man to be less critical in his judgments, and actions.

LAUGHTER & MIRTH

לִשְׂחוֹק אָמַרְתִּי מְהוֹלָל וּלְשִׂמְחָה מַה־זֹּה עֹשָׂה

"I said of laughter, it is mad; and of mirth, what does it achieve (2:2)?"

King Solomon recognized that the need for accomplishment interferes with enjoyments. This explains why people cannot sustain a lifestyle of endless partying. It results in nothing, frustrating man's innate need for accomplishment. *"...what does it achieve?"* teaches that a person has a need for accomplishment and that these attitudes and pursuits don't offer that fulfillment.

51

Rashi holds that there are three attacks on the life of drinking and laughter:

1) Once you block out reality through drunkenness, you harm yourself: *"this too is futile."*

2) The need for accomplishment forces man to anticipate whether his chosen lifestyle will lead to success. And when man sees no accomplishments due to his drinking, which derails his progress, he despises this life: *"and of mirth, what does it achieve?"*

3) *"I said of laughter, it is mad"* is the reaction to an attempt at playing with reality so as not to deal with stark reality. The joke or laughter cannot exist without the pain of reality. A joke will last only as long as the pain in reality lasts. Once the pain is gone, there's nothing to escape from. So the enjoyment of the laughter is not a pure enjoyment. It's only a negation of pain.

COMBINED PURSUITS

תַּרְתִּי בְלִבִּי לִמְשׁוֹךְ בַּיַּיִן אֶת־בְּשָׂרִי וְלִבִּי נֹהֵג
בַּחָכְמָה וְלֶאֱחֹז בְּסִכְלוּת עַד אֲשֶׁר־אֶרְאֶה אֵי־
זֶה טוֹב לִבְנֵי הָאָדָם אֲשֶׁר יַעֲשׂוּ תַּחַת הַשָּׁמַיִם
מִסְפַּר יְמֵי חַיֵּיהֶם

*"I sought in my heart to give myself to wine, yet guiding
my heart with wisdom and to seize folly, until I might
see which is good for the sons of men that they should
do under the heavens the number of the days of their
lives (2:3)."*

The king realized that wisdom and drink were not enjoyable
lifestyles. Knowledge fails to offer happiness: you realize that

the enjoyments aren't really enjoyable. And drinking fails to offer happiness because it denies the satisfaction of your desires.[15]

So he now tries to embrace both, adding folly as well. King Solomon concludes to make a compromise. But the compromise isn't the end of the line, because we see the king says, *"until I might see which is good."* These words refer to analytical wisdom as opposed to the wisdom where you mainly keep yourself in a state where the emotions won't take over and subdue one's self. King Solomon realizes that this path too will keep him unhappy. But there is one more possibility: the life of the instincts in their sophisticated form, i.e., "sophistication." This was the next trial, *"to seize folly."*

---

15) Man is incapacitated while drunk. In that state, he cannot attain desires or basic needs.

SOPHISTICATION

הִגְדַּלְתִּי מַעֲשָׂי בָּנִיתִי לִי בָּתִּים נָטַעְתִּי לִי כְּרָ־
מִים   עָשִׂיתִי לִי גַּנּוֹת וּפַרְדֵּסִים וְנָטַעְתִּי בָהֶם
עֵץ כָּל־פֶּרִי
עָשִׂיתִי לִי בְּרֵכוֹת מָיִם לְהַשְׁקוֹת מֵהֶם
יַעַר צוֹמֵחַ עֵצִים
קָנִיתִי עֲבָדִים וּשְׁפָחוֹת וּבְנֵי־בַיִת הָיָה לִי גַּם
מִקְנֶה בָקָר וָצֹאן הַרְבֵּה הָיָה לִי
מִכֹּל שֶׁהָיוּ לְפָנַי בִּירוּשָׁלָ͏ִם
כָּנַסְתִּי לִי גַּם־כֶּסֶף וְזָהָב וּסְגֻלַּת מְלָכִים וְהַמְּ־
דִינוֹת עָשִׂיתִי לִי שָׁרִים וְשָׁרוֹת וְתַעֲנֻגוֹת בְּנֵי
הָאָדָם שִׁדָּה וְשִׁדּוֹת

55

"I made great works for myself; I built houses; I planted vineyards. I made gardens and orchards, and I planted trees in them of all kinds of fruits. I made pools of water, to water with it a forest of growing trees. I acquired servants and maidens, and household members; also I had great possessions of herds and flocks, more than all who were in Jerusalem before me. I gathered also silver and gold, and the treasure of kings and of the provinces; I set for myself servants and maid servants, and the delight of men, chariots and wagons (2:4-8)."

These five verses describe the king's degree of indulgence, answering any question whether he truly attempted to enjoy the luxuries and sophistications that wealth offers. He intended to leave no stone unturned in his exploration of happiness.

WEALTH

וְגָדַלְתִּי וְהוֹסַפְתִּי מִכֹּל שֶׁהָיָה לְפָנַי בִּירוּשָׁלָ‍ם
אַף חָכְמָתִי עָמְדָה לִּי

"And I was great, and increased more than all whom preceded me in Jerusalem; but my wisdom remained with me (2:9)."

"...but my wisdom remained with me." King Solomon retained his objectivity, despite the blinding prestige men imagine when they are successful.

The Rabbis say this refers to the wisdom he learned with

anger.[16] The reason why אַף (anger) is necessary here is due to the overpowering emotion to cave to the feeling of sophistication.[17] Anger was needed to overpower this emotion.

Maimonides says that one cannot acquire Torah through laziness; learning must be through energetic attempts.

---

16) A play on the word אף which can mean "but" or "anger."
17) Anger helps one strengthen his intellect over his emotions. This is treated at length in the chapter entitled *The Psyche & Perfection.*

INDULGENCE

וְכֹל אֲשֶׁר שָׁאֲלוּ עֵינַי לֹא אָצַלְתִּי מֵהֶם
לֹא־מָנַעְתִּי אֶת־לִבִּי מִכָּל־שִׂמְחָה
כִּי־לִבִּי שָׂמֵחַ מִכָּל־עֲמָלִי
וְזֶה־הָיָה חֶלְקִי מִכָּל־עֲמָלִי

*"And whatever my eyes desired I kept not from them;
I did not restrain my heart from any joy, for my heart
rejoiced in all my labor, and this was my portion of all
my labor (2:10)."*

"...for my heart rejoiced in all my labor." He enjoyed the labor. It
satisfied the real need for accomplishment. But mere possession of products and wealth provided no enjoyment.[18]

---

18) When man labors towards a goal, there is happiness in the process of accomplishing.
Man's natural ambition is being satisfied. But subsequent to completing his labors, the mere
possession of his products does not satisfy any innate psychological need. This is contrary to
the popular view that possessions afford man real satisfaction. Happiness occurs only when
a real need is addressed, and not when one chases fantasies.

SOPHISTICATION

וּפָנִיתִי אֲנִי בְּכָל־מַעֲשַׂי שֶׁעָשׂוּ יָדַי וּבֶעָמָל
שֶׁעָמַלְתִּי לַעֲשׂוֹת וְהִנֵּה הַכֹּל הֶבֶל וּרְעוּת רוּחַ
וְאֵין יִתְרוֹן תַּחַת הַשָּׁמֶשׁ

*"Then I looked at all the works that my hands had
done, and at the labor that I had labored to do; and,
behold, all was futile and a vexation of spirit, and there
was nothing additional under the sun (2:11)."*

After King Solomon acquired servants, a household, luxurious living, cultivated landscapes, vehicles, wealth and other amenities of the rich and sophisticated lifestyle, he was

depressed. This is because sophistication is man's removal from the instincts. The king calls this sophistication *"futile and a vexation of spirit."* Futile, because there is nothing in life to substantiate this feeling of importance. A *"vexation of spirit"* means depression, that which leads to unhappiness. Since the instincts are being thwarted and are not being satisfied, this results in frustration.[19] Feeling important stems from the need[20] for importance, and not from reality.

"Then I looked at all the works that my hands had done." The labors were depressing, empty and not realistic. When a person involves himself in a worthless pursuit such as trying to be the successful businessman, his reality principle knows this to be false. It's a mere facade. But he must suppress this reality. And once there is a suppression, there is naturally an unsatisfied part existing within him. So he won't be happy.

This ends Rabbi Chait's initial lectures from the early 1970s. The following chapters are lectures given during 1986 and 1987 which include further insights on the first chapter and address most of the remaining chapters of Koheles.

---

19) A sophisticate restrains his base drives, acting with refined mannerism such as formal dining etiquette, adopted in finishing schools. Man's base instinct is to eat without restraint, freely satisfying the appetitive drive. But when this drive is restrained in order to appear refined in company, that drive undergoes frustration.
20) A need of the ego. Ego is an essential psychological component, and has its place in a Torah lifestyle. But often, man satisfies his ego drive in a futile or destructive fashion. Thus, many needs should not be satisfied as man typically wishes.

Part II: Contradictions
INTRODUCTION

The problems with Koheles are due to the contradictory[21] nature of the book: many verses conflict with others. The purpose of the following lectures is to show the underlying philosophy of Koheles. King Solomon hides his philosophy within the contradiction, but the solutions lie right next to the contradictions.

---

21) Rabbi Chait explained that King Solomon employed contradictions in order to keep the ideas hidden for the wise men to discern. Perhaps the use of apparent contradictions is the king's method of enabling this discernment. Mere facts do not engage the mind. But when the wise reader detects statements like "wisdom is pain," and then reads "nothing compares to wisdom," he is driven to resolve the contradiction. Primarily, he must determine if wisdom is a benefit or not. Once he determines its benefit, he must interpret the other verse explaining "when and why" wisdom is pain. Uncovering the verse's clues, he derives what considerations render wisdom to partake of contradictory values, resolving the contradiction. The reader then arrives at the intended lesson, which would be lost, had he not been prodded to resolve a contradiction.

He discusses knowledge, happiness, success, justice, ethics and least mentioned, *Olam Haba*, the Afterlife. In all topics, the solutions are interspersed.

Verses will be followed by summaries, isolating the succinct message of each verse. This method of presentation will help the reader grasp the precise contradictions. Part III will provide resolutions.

KNOWLEDGE

וְנָתַתִּי אֶת־לִבִּי לִדְרוֹשׁ וְלָתוּר בַּחָכְמָה עַל כָּל־
אֲשֶׁר נַעֲשָׂה תַּחַת הַשָּׁמָיִם הוּא | עִנְיַן רָע נָתַן
אֱלֹהִים לִבְנֵי הָאָדָם לַעֲנוֹת בּוֹ

"And I applied my heart to inquire and search with wisdom on all that is performed under the heaven; it is an evil matter God gave to the sons of man to afflict him (1:13)."

If knowledge is evil, why does he engage it? A contradiction.

כִּי בְּרֹב חָכְמָה רָב־כָּעַס
וְיוֹסִיף דַּעַת יוֹסִיף מַכְאוֹב

*"For in much wisdom there is much anger, and he that
increases knowledge increases sorrow (1:18)."*

Wisdom results in pain.

הֶחָכָם עֵינָיו בְּרֹאשׁוֹ וְהַכְּסִיל בַּחֹשֶׁךְ הוֹלֵךְ
וְיָדַעְתִּי גַם־אָנִי שֶׁמִּקְרֶה אֶחָד יִקְרֶה אֶת־כֻּלָּם

*"The wise man's eyes are in his head, but the fool walks
in darkness; and I myself perceived also that one event
happens to them all (2:14)."*

Even though wisdom is good, *"eyes are in his head,"* you end
up the same as a fool. Wisdom does not shield the wise man
from death.

כִּי מַה־יּוֹתֵר לֶחָכָם מִן־הַכְּסִיל
מַה־לֶּעָנִי יוֹדֵעַ לַהֲלֹךְ נֶגֶד הַחַיִּים

*"For what advantage has the wise man over the fool?
What has the poor man who knows how to walk among
the living (6:8)?"*

There is no advantage in being a wise person.

הַחָכְמָה תָּעֹז לֶחָכָם מֵעֲשָׂרָה שַׁלִּיטִים
אֲשֶׁר הָיוּ בָּעִיר

*"Wisdom strengthens the wise more than ten rulers who
are in the city (7:19)."*

Now King Solomon contradicts himself, saying wisdom is
strength.

מִי־כְּהֶחָכָם וּמִי יוֹדֵעַ פֵּשֶׁר דָּבָר
חָכְמַת אָדָם תָּאִיר פָּנָיו וְעֹז פָּנָיו יְשֻׁנֶּא

*"Who is like the wise man? and who knows the mean-
ing of a matter? A man's wisdom makes his face shine,
and the boldness of his face is changed (8:1)."*

Wisdom is incomparable.

דִּבְרֵי חֲכָמִים כַּדָּרְבֹנוֹת וּכְמַשְׂמְרוֹת נְטוּעִים
בַּעֲלֵי אֲסֻפּוֹת נִתְּנוּ מֵרֹעֶה אֶחָד

*"The words of the wise are like goads, and like nails
firmly fixed are the collected sayings, which are given
by one shepherd (12:11)."*

The words of a wise man are unshakable, like hammered
nails. They cannot be uprooted; they are true.

דִּבַּרְתִּי אֲנִי עִם־לִבִּי לֵאמֹר אֲנִי הִנֵּה הִגְדַּלְתִּי
וְהוֹסַפְתִּי חָכְמָה עַל כָּל־אֲשֶׁר־הָיָה לְפָנַי עַל־
יְרוּשָׁלָ͏ִם וְלִבִּי רָאָה הַרְבֵּה חָכְמָה וָדָעַת

"...and my heart has seen much of wisdom and knowledge (1:16)."

I saw much knowledge, it is a value.

כָּל־זֹה נִסִּיתִי בַחָכְמָה אָמַרְתִּי אֶחְכָּמָה וְהִיא
רְחוֹקָה מִמֶּנִּי

"All this have I proved by wisdom; I said, I will be wise; but it was far from me (7:23)."

He is in contradiction even with his personal knowledge.

HAPPINESS

הֲבֵל הֲבָלִים אָמַר קֹהֶלֶת הֲבֵל הֲבָלִים הַכֹּל
הָבֶל   מַה־יִּתְרוֹן לָאָדָם בְּכָל־עֲמָלוֹ שֶׁיַּעֲמֹל
תַּחַת הַשָּׁמֶשׁ   דּוֹר הֹלֵךְ וְדוֹר בָּא וְהָאָרֶץ
לְעוֹלָם עֹמָדֶת

*"Vanity of vanities, said Koheles, vanity of vanities; all
is vanity. What gains a man from all his labor at which
he labors under the sun? One generation passes away,
and another generation comes; but the earth abides for
ever (1:2-4)."*

There is no happiness; all is futile.

כָּל־הַדְּבָרִים יְגֵעִים לֹא־יוּכַל אִישׁ לְדַבֵּר לֹא־
תִשְׂבַּע עַיִן לִרְאוֹת וְלֹא־תִמָּלֵא אֹזֶן מִשְּׁמֹעַ

*"All things are wearisome; man cannot utter it; the eye
is not satisfied with seeing, nor the ear filled from hearing (1:8)."*

There is no satisfaction.

אָמַרְתִּי אֲנִי בְּלִבִּי לְכָה־נָּא אֲנַסְּכָה בְשִׂמְחָה
וּרְאֵה בְטוֹב וְהִנֵּה גַם־הוּא הָבֶל

*"I said in my heart, 'Come now, I will try you with
mirth, therefore enjoy pleasure'; and, behold, this also
is vanity (2:1)."*

I tried to be happy, but it's nonsense and impossible.

גַם כָּל־הָאָדָם אֲשֶׁר נָתַן־לוֹ הָאֱלֹהִים עֹשֶׁר
וּנְכָסִים וְהִשְׁלִיטוֹ לֶאֱכֹל מִמֶּנּוּ וְלָשֵׂאת אֶת־
חֶלְקוֹ וְלִשְׂמֹחַ בַּעֲמָלוֹ זֹה מַתַּת אֱלֹהִים הִיא
כִּי לֹא הַרְבֵּה יִזְכֹּר אֶת־יְמֵי חַיָּיו כִּי הָאֱלֹהִים
מַעֲנֶה בְּשִׂמְחַת לִבּוֹ

*"Every man also to whom God has given riches and
wealth, and has given him power to eat of it, and to
take his portion, and to rejoice in his labor; this is the
gift of God. For he shall not much remember the days of
his life, in which God provides him with the joy of his
heart (5:18,19)."*

If a person has his needs, he is happy. But in verse 5:19 King Solomon says that one won't remember the days of his life. He contradicts verse 5:17, "...*enjoy the good of all his labor in which he toils under the sun during the number of the days, which God gave him.*"

אִישׁ אֲשֶׁר יִתֶּן־לוֹ הָאֱלֹהִים עֹשֶׁר וּנְכָסִים
וְכָבוֹד וְאֵינֶנּוּ חָסֵר לְנַפְשׁוֹ | מִכֹּל אֲשֶׁר־יִתְאַוֶּה
וְלֹא־יַשְׁלִיטֶנּוּ הָאֱלֹהִים לֶאֱכֹל מִמֶּנּוּ כִּי אִישׁ
נָכְרִי יֹאכְלֶנּוּ זֶה הֶבֶל וָחֳלִי רָע הוּא

"A man to whom God has given riches, wealth, and honor, so that he lacks nothing for his soul of all that he desires, yet God does not give him power to eat of it, but a stranger eats it; this is vanity, and it is an evil disease (6:2)."

There is no satisfaction.

טוֹב לָלֶכֶת אֶל־בֵּית־אֵבֶל מִלֶּכֶת אֶל־בֵּית
מִשְׁתֶּה בַּאֲשֶׁר הוּא סוֹף כָּל־הָאָדָם
וְהַחַי יִתֵּן אֶל־לִבּוֹ

לֵב חֲכָמִים בְּבֵית אֵבֶל
וְלֵב כְּסִילִים בְּבֵית שִׂמְחָה

"It is better to go to the house of mourning, than to go to the house of feasting; for that is the end of all men; and the living will lay it to his heart (7:2)."

"The heart of the wise is in the house of mourning; but the heart of fools is in the house of mirth (7:4)."

The reality of death diminishes pleasures.

וְשִׁבַּ֨חְתִּי אֲנִי֙ אֶת־הַשִּׂמְחָ֔ה אֲשֶׁ֥ר אֵֽין־ט֖וֹב
לָֽאָדָם֙ תַּ֣חַת הַשֶּׁ֔מֶשׁ כִּ֛י אִם־לֶֽאֱכֹ֥ל וְלִשְׁתּ֖וֹת
וְלִשְׂמ֑וֹחַ וְה֞וּא יִלְוֶ֣נּוּ בַעֲמָל֗וֹ יְמֵ֤י חַיָּיו֙ אֲשֶׁר־
נָֽתַן־ל֥וֹ הָאֱלֹהִ֖ים תַּ֥חַת הַשָּֽׁמֶשׁ

"And I commended mirth, because a man has no better thing under the sun, than to eat, and to drink, and to be merry; for this will go with him in his labor during the days of his life, which God gives him under the sun (8:15)."

Eat, drink and be merry for this is happiness. He contradicts himself in other verses suggesting there is no happiness.

JUSTICE

אָמַרְתִּי אֲנִי בְּלִבִּי אֶת־הַצַּדִּיק וְאֶת־הָרָשָׁע
יִשְׁפֹּט הָאֱלֹהִים כִּי־עֵת לְכָל־חֵפֶץ וְעַל כָּל
הַמַּעֲשֶׂה שָׁם

"I said in my heart, God shall judge the righteous and the wicked; for there is a time there for every purpose and for every work (3:17)."

There is justice.

כִּי מִקְרֶה בְנֵי־הָאָדָם וּמִקְרֶה הַבְּהֵמָה
וּמִקְרֶה אֶחָד לָהֶם כְּמוֹת זֶה כֵּן מוֹת זֶה
וְרוּחַ אֶחָד לַכֹּל וּמוֹתַר הָאָדָם מִן־הַבְּהֵמָה אָיִן
כִּי הַכֹּל הָבֶל

*"For that which befalls the sons of men befalls beasts;
one thing befalls them both; as the one dies, so dies the
other; They have all one breath; so that a man has no
preeminence above a beast; for all is vanity (3:19)."*

Man is equal to animal. Where's the justice?

וְשַׁבְתִּי אֲנִי וָאֶרְאֶה אֶת־כָּל־הָעֲשֻׁקִים אֲשֶׁר
נַעֲשִׂים תַּחַת הַשָּׁמֶשׁ וְהִנֵּה | דִּמְעַת הָעֲשֻׁקִים
וְאֵין לָהֶם מְנַחֵם וּמִיַּד עֹשְׁקֵיהֶם כֹּחַ
וְאֵין לָהֶם מְנַחֵם

*"So I returned, and considered all the oppressions that are
done under the sun; and behold the tears of such as were oppressed, and they had no comforter; and on the side of their
oppressors there was power; but they had no comforter (4:1)."*

No justice for the oppressed.

יֶשׁ־הֶבֶל אֲשֶׁר נַעֲשָׂה עַל־הָאָרֶץ אֲשֶׁר | יֵשׁ
צַדִּיקִים אֲשֶׁר מַגִּיעַ אֲלֵהֶם כְּמַעֲשֵׂה הָרְשָׁעִים
וְיֵשׁ רְשָׁעִים שֶׁמַּגִּיעַ אֲלֵהֶם כְּמַעֲשֵׂה הַצַּדִּיקִים
אָמַרְתִּי שֶׁגַּם־זֶה הָבֶל

*"There is a vanity which is done upon the earth; that
there are just men, to whom it happens according to the
deeds of the wicked; again, there are wicked men, to
whom it happens according to the deeds of the righteous;
I said that this also is vanity (8:14)."*

There is no justice.

כִּי אֶת־כָּל־מַעֲשֶׂה הָאֱלֹהִים יָבֵא בְמִשְׁפָּט עַל
כָּל־נֶעְלָם אִם־טוֹב וְאִם־רָע

*"For God shall bring every deed into judgment, with
every hidden thing, whether it is good, or whether it is
evil (12:14)."*

Every action is judged. There is justice; a contradiction.

ETHICS

תַּרְתִּי בְלִבִּי לִמְשׁוֹךְ בַּיַּיִן אֶת־בְּשָׂרִי וְלִבִּי נֹהֵג
בַּחָכְמָה וְלֶאֱחֹז בְּסִכְלוּת עַד אֲשֶׁר־אֶרְאֶה אֵי־
זֶה טוֹב לִבְנֵי הָאָדָם אֲשֶׁר יַעֲשׂוּ תַּחַת הַשָּׁמַיִם
מִסְפַּר יְמֵי חַיֵּיהֶם

*"I sought in my heart to give myself to wine, yet guiding
my heart with wisdom; and to lay hold on folly, until
I might see what was good for the sons of men, which
they should do under the heaven all the days of their
life (2:3)."*

Follow a life of folly.

אַל־תְּהִי צַדִּיק הַרְבֵּה וְאַל־תִּתְחַכַּם יוֹתֵר לָמָּה
תִּשּׁוֹמֵם   אַל־תִּרְשַׁע הַרְבֵּה וְאַל־תְּהִי סָכָל
לָמָּה תָמוּת בְּלֹא עִתֶּךָ

*"Do not be too righteous; nor make yourself too wise;
why should you destroy yourself? Do not be too wicked, nor be foolish; why should you die before your time
(7:16,17)?"*

Do not be too righteous or too foolish, but partake of both.

This conflicts with the previous verse.

SUCCESS

מַה־יִּתְרוֹן הָעוֹשֶׂה בַּאֲשֶׁר הוּא עָמֵל

"What gains has he who works in that in which he labors (3:9)?"

There is no benefit in labor.

וְגַם־זֹה רָעָה חוֹלָה כָּל־עֻמַּת שֶׁבָּא כֵּן יֵלֵךְ
וּמַה־יִּתְרוֹן לוֹ שֶׁיַּעֲמֹל לָרוּחַ

"And this also is a grievous evil, that inasmuch as he came, so shall he go; and what gains has he who has labored for the wind (5:15)?"

What is the purpose of working?

וְשָׂנֵאתִי אֲנִי אֶת־כָּל־עֲמָלִי שֶׁאֲנִי עָמֵל תַּחַת
הַשָּׁמֶשׁ שֶׁאַנִּיחֶנּוּ לָאָדָם שֶׁיִּהְיֶה אַחֲרָי
וּמִי יוֹדֵעַ הֶחָכָם יִהְיֶה אוֹ סָכָל וְיִשְׁלַט בְּכָל־
עֲמָלִי שֶׁעָמַלְתִּי וְשֶׁחָכַמְתִּי תַּחַת הַשָּׁמֶשׁ
גַּם־זֶה הָבֶל   וְסַבּוֹתִי אֲנִי לְיַאֵשׁ אֶת־לִבִּי עַל
כָּל־הֶעָמָל שֶׁעָמַלְתִּי תַּחַת הַשָּׁמֶשׁ
כִּי־יֵשׁ אָדָם שֶׁעֲמָלוֹ בְּחָכְמָה וּבְדַעַת וּבְכִשְׁרוֹן
וּלְאָדָם שֶׁלֹּא עָמַל־בּוֹ יִתְּנֶנּוּ חֶלְקוֹ גַּם־זֶה הֶבֶל
וְרָעָה רַבָּה

אִישׁ אֲשֶׁר יִתֶּן־לוֹ הָאֱלֹהִים עֹשֶׁר וּנְכָסִים
וְכָבוֹד וְאֵינֶנּוּ חָסֵר לְנַפְשׁוֹ | מִכֹּל אֲשֶׁר־יִתְאַוֶּה
וְלֹא־יַשְׁלִיטֶנּוּ הָאֱלֹהִים לֶאֱכֹל מִמֶּנּוּ כִּי אִישׁ
נָכְרִי יֹאכְלֶנּוּ זֶה הֶבֶל וָחֳלִי רָע הוּא

*"And I hated all my labor which I had taken under the
sun; because I should leave it to the man that shall be
after me. And who knows whether he shall be a wise
man or a fool? Yet he shall have rule over all my labor
in which I have labored, and in which I have showed
myself wise under the sun. This also is vanity. Therefore I went about to cause my heart to despair of all the
labor which I took under the sun. For there is a man
whose labor is with wisdom, and with knowledge, and
with skill; yet to a man that has not labored in it shall
he leave it for his portion. This also is vanity and a
great evil (2:18-21)."*

*"A man to whom God has given riches, wealth, and
honor, so that he lacks nothing for his soul of all that
he desires, yet God does not give him power to eat of
it, but a stranger eats it; this is vanity, and it is an evil
disease (6:2)."*

A person works and leaves it to another. Labor is futile.

וּפָנִיתִי אֲנִי בְּכָל־מַעֲשַׂי שֶׁעָשׂוּ יָדַי וּבֶעָמָל
שֶׁעָמַלְתִּי לַעֲשׂוֹת וְהִנֵּה הַכֹּל הֶבֶל וּרְעוּת רוּחַ
וְאֵין יִתְרוֹן תַּחַת הַשָּׁמֶשׁ

*"Then I looked at all the works that my hands had
done, and at the labor that I had labored to do; and,
behold, all was vanity and a stressful spirit, and there
was nothing to be gained under the sun (2:11)."*

All my work is useless; it provided no gain.

טוֹב שֵׁם מִשֶּׁמֶן טוֹב וְיוֹם הַמָּוֶת מִיּוֹם הִוָּלְדוֹ

*"A good name is better than precious oil; and the day of
death than the day of one's birth (7:1)."*

Of what use is a good name, as I won't be around to experience this?

81

כִּי־מִי אֲשֶׁר יְבָחַר [יְחֻבַּר] אֶל כָּל־הַחַיִּים יֵשׁ
בִּטָּחוֹן כִּי־לְכֶלֶב חַי הוּא טוֹב מִן־הָאַרְיֵה הַמֵּת

*"For to him who is joined to all the living there is hope;
for a living dog is better than a dead lion (9:4)."*

This means that success is limited by death. The very concept of success is ludicrous because it is inherently limited.

AFTERLIFE & IMMORTALITY

מִי יוֹדֵעַ רוּחַ בְּנֵי הָאָדָם הָעֹלָה הִיא לְמָעְלָה
וְרוּחַ הַבְּהֵמָה הַיֹּרֶדֶת הִיא לְמַטָּה לָאָרֶץ

*"Who knows that the spirit of man goes upward, and
the spirit of the beast that goes downward to the earth
(3:21)?"*

One occurrence happens to man and animal. Everything
came from the Earth and everything returns to the Earth. Most
men don't know what's going to happen after death.

וְרָאִיתִי כִּי אֵין טוֹב מֵאֲשֶׁר יִשְׂמַח הָאָדָם
בְּמַעֲשָׂיו כִּי־הוּא חֶלְקוֹ כִּי מִי יְבִיאֶנּוּ לִרְאוֹת
בְּמֶה שֶׁיִּהְיֶה אַחֲרָיו

*"So I saw that there is nothing better, than that a
man should rejoice in his work; for that is his portion;
For who can bring him to see what shall be after him
(3:22)?"*

One might as well enjoy this world. Man's earthly existence
is praised over death.

כֹּל אֲשֶׁר תִּמְצָא יָדְךָ לַעֲשׂוֹת בְּכֹחֲךָ עֲשֵׂה כִּי
אֵין מַעֲשֶׂה וְחֶשְׁבּוֹן וְדַעַת וְחָכְמָה בִּשְׁאוֹל
אֲשֶׁר אַתָּה הֹלֵךְ שָׁמָּה

*"Whatever your hand finds to do, do it with your
strength; for there is no work, nor scheme, nor knowledge, nor wisdom, in the grave to which you are going
(9:10)."*

The afterlife doesn't exist. Not only is there no physical, but
no intelligence as well.

Chapter 12 deals with man's deterioration. Man reaches a point where he doesn't desire life. The city deteriorating is a metaphor for man:

וּזְכֹר אֶת־בּוֹרְאֶיךָ בִּימֵי בְּחוּרֹתֶיךָ עַד אֲשֶׁר לֹא־
יָבֹאוּ יְמֵי הָרָעָה וְהִגִּיעוּ שָׁנִים אֲשֶׁר תֹּאמַר אֵין־
לִי בָהֶם חֵפֶץ   עַד אֲשֶׁר לֹא־תֶחְשַׁךְ הַשֶּׁמֶשׁ
וְהָאוֹר וְהַיָּרֵחַ וְהַכּוֹכָבִים וְשָׁבוּ הֶעָבִים אַחַר
הַגָּשֶׁם   בַּיּוֹם שֶׁיָּזֻעוּ שֹׁמְרֵי הַבַּיִת וְהִתְעַוְּתוּ
אַנְשֵׁי הֶחָיִל וּבָטְלוּ הַטֹּחֲנוֹת כִּי מִעֵטוּ וְחָשְׁ־
כוּ הָרֹאוֹת בָּאֲרֻבּוֹת   וְסֻגְּרוּ דְלָתַיִם בַּשּׁוּק
בִּשְׁפַל קוֹל הַטַּחֲנָה וְיָקוּם לְקוֹל הַצִּפּוֹר וְיִשַּׁחוּ
כָּל־בְּנוֹת הַשִּׁיר   גַּם מִגָּבֹהַּ יִרָאוּ וְחַתְחַ־
תִּים בַּדֶּרֶךְ וְיָנֵאץ הַשָּׁקֵד וְיִסְתַּבֵּל הֶחָגָב וְתָפֵר
הָאֲבִיּוֹנָה כִּי־הֹלֵךְ הָאָדָם אֶל־בֵּית עוֹלָמוֹ וְסָבְבוּ
בַשּׁוּק הַסּוֹפְדִים   עַד אֲשֶׁר לֹא־יֵרָחֵק
[יֵרָתֵק] חֶבֶל הַכֶּסֶף וְתָרֻץ גֻּלַּת הַזָּהָב וְתִשָּׁבֶר
כַּד עַל־הַמַּבּוּעַ וְנָרֹץ הַגַּלְגַּל אֶל־הַבּוֹר   וְיָשֹׁב
הֶעָפָר עַל־הָאָרֶץ כְּשֶׁהָיָה וְהָרוּחַ תָּשׁוּב אֶל־
הָאֱלֹהִים אֲשֶׁר נְתָנָהּ

85

"Remember now your Creator in the days of your youth, before the evil days come, and the years draw near, when you shall say, I have no pleasure in them; Before the sun, and the light, and the moon, and the stars are darkened, and the clouds return after the rain; In the day when the keepers of the house tremble, and the strong men bow themselves, and the grinders cease because they are few, and those who look out of the windows are dimmed, And the doors are shut on the streets, when the sound of the grinding is low, and one rises up at the voice of the bird, and all the daughters of song are brought low; Also when they are afraid of that which is high, and fears are in the way, and the almond tree blossoms, and the grasshopper drags itself along, and desire fails; because man goes to his eternal home, and the mourners go about the streets; Before the silver cord is removed[22], or the golden bowl is broken[23], or the pitcher is broken at the fountain, or the wheel broken at the cistern. And the dust returns to the earth as it was; and the spirit returns to God who gave it (12:1-7)."

But in verse 12:7 he says the spirit returns to God, indicating that he does believe in the Afterlife. A contradiction.

In summary, King Solomon appears to contradict himself on matters of knowledge, ethics, happiness, justice, success and the afterlife. In the following chapters, Rabbi Chait resolves many of these apparent contradictions and lectures on numerous themes throughout Koheles. At times, the resolutions are

---

22) A metaphor for the spinal cord (Rashi)
23) The male organ (Rashi)

brief and even a single sentence, which suffice to resolve the contradiction or present a concept. Other times, when necessary, the resolutions will be more elaborate.

Part III: Contradictions Resolved
KNOWLEDGE

כֹּל אֲשֶׁר תִּמְצָא יָדְךָ לַעֲשׂוֹת בְּכֹחֲךָ עֲשֵׂה כִּי
אֵין מַעֲשֶׂה וְחֶשְׁבּוֹן וְדַעַת וְחָכְמָה בִּשְׁאוֹל
אֲשֶׁר אַתָּה הֹלֵךְ שָׁמָּה

"Whatever your hand finds to do, do it with your strength; for there is no work, nor scheme, nor knowledge, nor wisdom, in the grave to which you are going (9:10)."

The king does not reject the Afterlife. He means that man's fantasy of what knowledge will afford him doesn't exist in the grave. Man's fantasies are attached to his earthly existence.

When he realizes his mortality, he devalues knowledge, since knowledge was viewed as a means to immortality: mortality devalues knowledge. Verse 2:15 echoes this idea, *"Then said I in my heart, As it happens to the fool, so it happens even to me; and why was I then more wise? Then I said in my heart, that this also is vanity."* Meaning, it is the man who views wisdom merely as a tool for earthly objectives who says this. Since knowledge does not procure his immortality, he questions the value of knowledge. The king is echoing the foolish man who despises wisdom once he realizes it doesn't save him from the grave. Again, the king is not voicing his opinion, but that of the fool. This contradiction is resolved.

כִּי בְּרֹב חָכְמָה רָב־כָּעַס
וְיוֹסִיף דַּעַת יוֹסִיף מַכְאוֹב

"For in much wisdom there is much grief; and he that increases knowledge increases sorrow (1:18)."

The more reality man sees, the more he recognizes he can't be happy with what he wanted. His desires are exposed as useless, or incapable of providing the fantasies he sought, like immortality or prestige. But this is not a rejection of wisdom. It is a commentary on the foolish man who finally wakes up.

מִי־כְּהֶחָכָם וּמִי יוֹדֵעַ פֵּשֶׁר דָּבָר חָכְמַת אָדָם
תָּאִיר פָּנָיו וְעֹז פָּנָיו יְשֻׁנֶּא

"Who is like the wise man and who knows the meaning of a matter? A man's wisdom makes his face shine, and the boldness of his face is changed (8:1)."

King Solomon's personal view: nothing compares to wisdom.

KOHELES

HAPPINESS

וְשִׁבַּחְתִּי אֲנִי אֶת־הַשִּׂמְחָה אֲשֶׁר אֵין־טוֹב
לָאָדָם תַּחַת הַשֶּׁמֶשׁ כִּי אִם־לֶאֱכֹל וְלִשְׁתּוֹת
וְלִשְׂמוֹחַ וְהוּא יִלְוֶנּוּ בַעֲמָלוֹ יְמֵי חַיָּיו אֲשֶׁר־
נָתַן־לוֹ הָאֱלֹהִים תַּחַת הַשָּׁמֶשׁ

"And I commended mirth, because a man has no better thing under the sun than to eat, and to drink, and to be merry; for this will go with him in his labor during the days of his life[24], which God gives him under the sun (8:15)."

Man must partake of a happy existence.

---

24) Notice the king repeats "his life." This stresses that the real enjoyments "during" life are worthwhile. As those are matters actually enjoyed – they are not fantasies. In contrast, an immortal fantasy like leaving wealth to another cannot be realized. For man is gone at the moment his wealth is bequeathed: *"And who knows whether he shall be a wise man or a fool, yet he shall have rule over all my labor in which I have labored (2:19)."*

אֶת־הַכֹּל עָשָׂה יָפֶה בְעִתּוֹ גַּם אֶת־הָעֹלָם נָתַן
בְּלִבָּם מִבְּלִי אֲשֶׁר לֹא־יִמְצָא הָאָדָם אֶת
הַמַּעֲשֶׂה אֲשֶׁר־עָשָׂה הָאֱלֹהִים מֵרֹאשׁ וְעַד־סוֹף
יָדַעְתִּי כִּי אֵין טוֹב בָּם כִּי אִם־לִשְׂמוֹחַ וְלַעֲשׂוֹת
טוֹב בְּחַיָּיו   וְגַם כָּל־הָאָדָם שֶׁיֹּאכַל וְשָׁתָה
וְרָאָה טוֹב בְּכָל־עֲמָלוֹ מַתַּת אֱלֹהִים הִיא

*"He has made every thing beautiful in his time; also
he has set the world in their heart, so that no man can
find out the work which God has made from the beginning to the end. I know that there is nothing better for
them, than to rejoice, and to do good in his life. And also
that it is the gift of God that every man should eat and
drink, and see the good of all his labor (3:11-13)."*

The only way to enjoy life is to abandon the fantasy of immortality. Then, man can value the here and now. One's happiness should be without ego satisfaction, *"the gift of God."*[25]

וְרָאִיתִי כִּי אֵין טוֹב מֵאֲשֶׁר יִשְׂמַח הָאָדָם בְּמַ־
עֲשָׂיו כִּי־הוּא חֶלְקוֹ כִּי מִי יְבִיאֶנּוּ לִרְאוֹת בְּמֶה
שֶׁיִּהְיֶה אַחֲרָיו

*"So I saw that there is nothing better, than that a man
should rejoice in his work; for that is his portion; for
who can bring him to see what shall be after him (3:22)?"*

Happiness shouldn't be tied to what occurs afterwards.

25) Only with this perspective does man free himself from his feeling of success, and can
appreciate it as external to his accomplishments, a "gift."

JUSTICE

אָמַרְתִּי אֲנִי בְּלִבִּי אֶת־הַצַּדִּיק וְאֶת־הָרָשָׁע
יִשְׁפֹּט הָאֱלֹהִים כִּי־עֵת לְכָל־חֵפֶץ וְעַל כָּל
הַמַּעֲשֶׂה שָׁם

"I said in my heart, God shall judge the righteous and the wicked; for there is a time there for every purpose and for every work (3:17)."

God judges fairly.

וְשַׁבְתִּי אֲנִי וָאֶרְאֶה אֶת־כָּל־הָעֲשֻׁקִים אֲשֶׁר
נַעֲשִׂים תַּחַת הַשָּׁמֶשׁ וְהִנֵּה | דִּמְעַת הָעֲשֻׁקִים
וְאֵין לָהֶם מְנַחֵם וּמִיַּד עֹשְׁקֵיהֶם כֹּחַ וְאֵין לָהֶם
מְנַחֵם

*"So I returned, and considered all the oppressions that
are done under the sun; and behold the tears of such as
were oppressed, and they had no comforter; and on the
side of their oppressors there was power; but they had
no comforter (4:1)."*

There is injustice for the oppressed.

יֶשׁ־הֶבֶל אֲשֶׁר נַעֲשָׂה עַל־הָאָרֶץ אֲשֶׁר | יֵשׁ
צַדִּיקִים אֲשֶׁר מַגִּיעַ אֲלֵהֶם כְּמַעֲשֵׂה הָרְשָׁעִים
וְיֵשׁ רְשָׁעִים שֶׁמַּגִּיעַ אֲלֵהֶם כְּמַעֲשֵׂה הַצַּדִּיקִים
אָמַרְתִּי שֶׁגַּם־זֶה הָבֶל

*"There is a vanity which is done upon the earth; that
there are just men, to whom it happens according to the
deeds of the wicked; again, there are wicked men, to
whom it happens according to the deeds of the righteous;
I said that this also is vanity (8:14)."*

The king seems to say there is no reward for righteous people. How do we answer these contradictions? Insofar as man
views these questions from a material framework, he won't
find an answer. Meaning, if one views "the good" as physical
security, these verses support questions on God's justice.

However, the true good God intends for man, and what man should value, is not temporal earthly life. True goodness is what affects our souls; our eternal element. Again we see how man's immortality fantasy tells him Earth is all that exists, so he values and devalues based on his assessment of his earthly successes, be it fortune, fame, or health.

רְאֵה חַיִּים עִם־אִשָּׁה אֲשֶׁר־אָהַבְתָּ כָּל־יְמֵי
חַיֵּי הֶבְלֶךָ אֲשֶׁר נָתַן־לְךָ תַּחַת הַשֶּׁמֶשׁ כֹּל יְמֵי
הֶבְלֶךָ כִּי הוּא חֶלְקְךָ בַּחַיִּים וּבַעֲמָלְךָ אֲשֶׁר
אַתָּה עָמֵל תַּחַת הַשָּׁמֶשׁ

"Live joyfully with the wife whom you love all the days of the life of your vanity, which he has given you under the sun, all the days of your vanity; for that is your portion in life, and in your labor in which you labor under the sun (9:9)."

If a person has the true ideas, no matter how little wealth he has and no matter what befalls him, he'll be happy. Genuine happiness is derived from living in line with truth and appreciating God's wisdom. Some of the Rabbis were extremely poor, but they were also extremely happy in their Torah lives. However, if man is tied to a physical life, he won't be happy. The Talmud[26] teaches that children, income, and one's lifespan aren't due to merits, but to chance.[27]

---

26) Moade Kattan 28a
27) The point being that man is not correct in questioning God's justice about these three

Regarding personal knowledge, the king had more knowledge than anyone. This refers to factual knowledge. But in terms of "feeling" smarter, he remarked, *I said I would become wise, but it was far from me (7:23)."* When he tried to satisfy the emotion of attaining a self-image of a "wise man", it fell short. Like all fantasies, the reality must fall short of how we imagine we will feel. Fantasies are perfect. We concoct a flawless image in our minds, and add to the impossibility of attaining that fantasy the feeling they will endure endlessly. But reality cannot provide this.

The main idea of Koheles is a breakdown of immortality. There are occurrences which ruin long-term plans and fantasies: *"...the righteous, and the wise, and their deeds, are in the hand of God...(9:11)"*

---

matters, for they are not granted based on our righteousness. This explains why the Rabbis who lived in poverty didn't complain. Additionally, these matters cannot remove a person from pursuing true happiness through studying God's Torah and His universe; our true objective.

AFTERLIFE & IMMORTALITY

מִי יוֹדֵעַ רוּחַ בְּנֵי הָאָדָם הָעֹלָה הִיא לְמָעְלָה
וְרוּחַ הַבְּהֵמָה הַיֹּרֶדֶת הִיא לְמַטָּה לָאָרֶץ

*"Who knows the spirit of man, that goes upward, and
the spirit of the beast that goes downward to the Earth
(3:21)?"*

The king did not say הָעֹלָה (ha-olah) *"if it goes up"*, which
would question if the soul endures. Rather, he says הָעֹלָה (haw-
olah) *"that goes up."* Thus, the king was not questioning whether
the Afterlife is real. He knew it was so.[28] He was saying "Which

---

28) His intent is to say, *"Which men know the Afterlife is a truth?"* Meaning, it is true, but so
few men know of this, or live with this conviction.

people are convinced in the truth of the Afterlife?" This is the meaning of *"Who knows the spirit of man, that goes upward..."* This removes the question of whether King Solomon believed in the Afterlife. He clearly affirms its truth.

וְרָאִיתִי כִּי אֵין טוֹב מֵאֲשֶׁר יִשְׂמַח הָאָדָם
בְּמַעֲשָׂיו כִּי־הוּא חֶלְקוֹ כִּי מִי יְבִיאֶנּוּ לִרְאוֹת
בְּמֶה שֶׁיִּהְיֶה אַחֲרָיו

"So I saw that there is nothing better, than that a man should rejoice in his work; for that is his portion; for who can bring him to see what shall be after him (3:22)?"

This verse deals with the idea that one should be concerned with only the here and now, and not the Afterlife. In this verse, King Solomon depicts man's false view. Very few men have knowledge about the soul after death. The king means to say that man's fantasy of immortality causes this belief, that all man has is an earthly existence. This is not an opinion based on knowledge.[29]

The king is not concerned with merely what the good is, but also with understanding human motivation. Here, man's fantasy of immortality motivates him to view his earthly existence

_____

29) Many times in Koheles (3:19, 9:4, 9:7), King Solomon voices the opinion of the populous, and not his own opinion. Knowing this fact, we remove many questions. By voicing the popular (ignorant) view of mankind, he gains man's attention, thereby enabling man to hear his rejection of their unexamined views.

as his only existence. Most men are unsure that the soul does in fact continue. Again, the king was not questioning this. He means "Who among men know that the soul truly continues?" And based on this doubt among most men, verse 3:22 expresses their natural conclusion, "...*there is nothing better, than that a man should rejoice in his work; for that is his portion...*"

King Solomon maintained that the most detrimental part of man is his ego, "גַּם אֶת־הָעֹלָם נָתַן בְּלִבָּם ; *Also the world He has placed in man's heart (3:11)."* This feeling prevents man from uncovering reality. The ego drive in man expresses itself through success, religion and knowledge. These are ways man feels he will achieve immortality.

Man's nature and his relationships to his objectives are such, that he targets goals which cannot be achieved in reality. His true objective is to attain immortality. That is why man is frustrated when he arrives at his goal: what he searched for doesn't exist.[30] He deluded himself that he was aspiring to attain fame or riches. In truth, he harbored an underlying desire for immortality.[31] Therefore, the riches cannot satisfy this fantasy, and he remains unhappy.

---

30) He is not immortal.
31) When, after decades of labor, man attains great wealth and fame, man is unsatisfied since these were not his true objectives. He was seeking immortality. Throughout life, he senses dissatisfaction and frustration, until in old age, he senses depression when he finally accepts his mortality.

Part IV: Themes of Koheles
PSYCHOLOGY

Ancient philosophers possessed true ideas, but they did not demonstrate how to incorporate these ideas into life. Koheles addresses not only philosophy, but also psychology. Without psychology, you cannot benefit from the ideas.

An example is one whose immortality fantasy encompasses immortal earthly life and physical pleasures. He is not in the position to question why evil happens to good people. Understanding the psychology at play, we appreciate why this is so. The questioner has distorted values, as he prioritizes the physical world. The good person who seems to be suffering from poverty for example, may not see as much evil in his life as the questioner who prioritizes riches to attain his pleasures. Thus, by understanding psychology, we grasp the philosophical aspects of happiness and justice.

Why did King Solomon have to go through the experiences to attain his knowledge? Couldn't he have simply pondered? No. Without going through the actual experiences, he wouldn't have seen the emotions' dynamics so as to know how to battle them. King Solomon was the only individual who could immerse in the pleasures without them affecting him, *"...but my wisdom remained with me (2:9)."*

WISDOM

וְנָתַתִּי אֶת־לִבִּי לִדְרוֹשׁ וְלָתוּר בַּחָכְמָה עַל כָּל־
אֲשֶׁר נַעֲשָׂה תַּחַת הַשָּׁמָיִם הוּא | עִנְיַן רָע נָתַן
אֱלֹהִים לִבְנֵי הָאָדָם לַעֲנוֹת בּוֹ

*"And I applied my heart to inquire and search with
wisdom on all that is performed under the heaven; it
is an evil matter God gave to the sons of man to afflict
him (1:13)."*

If wisdom is an evil matter, why did King Solomon investigate
with it?

Man has a task, to search out a philosophy by which to live.

Other creatures possess instincts which naturally determine
their actions. Man's task to search out a philosophy is something which is an evil matter because man has no natural means
which tell him how to live. He's walking in the dark. *"For in
much wisdom there is much grief; and he that increases knowledge
increases sorrow (1:18)."* Even the process itself is rough. The
more knowledge, the more pain. Verse 1:13 says the undertak-
ing of human investigation per se is a painful, and 1:18 deals
with the pains of actual investigation.

וּפָנִיתִי אֲנִי לִרְאוֹת חָכְמָה וְהוֹלֵלוֹת וְסִכְלוּת כִּי
מֶה הָאָדָם שֶׁיָּבוֹא אַחֲרֵי הַמֶּלֶךְ אֵת אֲשֶׁר־ |
כְּבָר עָשׂוּהוּ

*"And I turned myself to behold wisdom, and madness,
and folly; for what is man who comes after the king,
even that which has been already done (2:12)?"*

Man is given no right to choose what happiness is, even
though he's human. "Man came after the king" – after the
framework has been set up, man cannot change it. God laid
down how man functions and what is his design. Therefore
man must follow his design. Man's investigation cannot be
prejudiced by his drive for pleasure: man usually decides
where his happiness is depending upon where his energies lie.
Existentialists like this notion, that everything must con-

form to how they feel about things. They suggest that man's happiness must be in line with how he feels.

וְרָאִיתִי אָנִי שֶׁיֵּשׁ יִתְרוֹן לַחׇכְמָה מִן
הַסִּכְלוּת כִּיתְרוֹן הָאוֹר מִן־הַחֹשֶׁךְ הֶחָכָם
עֵינָיו בְּרֹאשׁוֹ וְהַכְּסִיל בַּחֹשֶׁךְ הוֹלֵךְ וְיָדַעְתִּי גַם־
אָנִי שֶׁמִּקְרֶה אֶחָד יִקְרֶה אֶת־כֻּלָּם

"Then I saw that wisdom excels folly, like light excels darkness. The wise man's eyes are in his head; but the fool walks in darkness...(2:13,14)."

The king says that wisdom is best. But he doesn't say that it is happiness. All he says here is that there are practical benefits.

וְאָמַרְתִּי אֲנִי בְּלִבִּי כְּמִקְרֶה הַכְּסִיל גַּם־אֲנִי
יִקְרֵנִי וְלָמָּה חָכַמְתִּי אֲנִי אָז יֹתֵר וְדִבַּרְתִּי בְלִבִּי
שֶׁגַּם־זֶה הָבֶל כִּי אֵין זִכְרוֹן לֶחָכָם עִם־הַכְּסִיל
לְעוֹלָם בְּשֶׁכְּבָר הַיָּמִים הַבָּאִים הַכֹּל נִשְׁכָּח
וְאֵיךְ יָמוּת הֶחָכָם עִם־הַכְּסִיל

"Then said I in my heart, As it happens to the fool, so it happens even to me; and why was I then more wise? Then I said in my heart, that this also is vanity. For there is no remembrance of the wise more than of the fool forever; seeing that the days to come shall all be forgotten. And how dies the wise man just like the fool (2:15,16)?"

The king applies his search to wisdom and learns that man doesn't find the happiness in wisdom[32] for which he was searching. Frustrated emotions must have an outlet. The fantasy of immortality is gone. But something is left: "Perhaps my energies that were invested will have some reward or satisfaction" the king thinks. But even this he doesn't find.

וְשָׂנֵאתִי אֶת־הַחַיִּים כִּי רַע עָלַי הַמַּעֲשֶׂה
שֶׁנַּעֲשָׂה תַּחַת הַשָּׁמֶשׁ כִּי־הַכֹּל הֶבֶל וּרְעוּת
רוּחַ   וְשָׂנֵאתִי אֲנִי אֶת־כָּל־עֲמָלִי שֶׁאֲנִי עָמֵל
תַּחַת הַשָּׁמֶשׁ שֶׁאַנִּיחֶנּוּ לָאָדָם שֶׁיִּהְיֶה אַחֲרָי
וּמִי יוֹדֵעַ הֶחָכָם יִהְיֶה אוֹ סָכָל וְיִשְׁלַט בְּכָל־
עֲמָלִי שֶׁעָמַלְתִּי וְשֶׁחָכַמְתִּי תַּחַת הַשָּׁמֶשׁ
גַּם־זֶה הָבֶל

"Therefore I hated life; because the work that is done under the sun was grievous to me; for all is vanity and a stressful spirit. And I hated all my labor which I had taken under the sun; because I should leave it to the man that shall be after me. And who knows whether he shall be a wise man or a fool, yet he shall have rule over all my labor in which I have labored, and in which I have showed myself wise under the sun. This also is vanity (2:17-19)."

32) This dissatisfaction with wisdom is not because he didn't enjoy wisdom. The king already said there is nothing like wisdom. He is echoing the man who uses wisdom as a tool to attain immortality. "And how dies the wise man just like the fool?" expresses this man's disappointment when he confronts his mortality. He recognizes that his fantasy that wisdom would somehow secure immortality, is false. He questions wisdom's benefit, since it doesn't save him from the grave. But the person who studies Torah and nature purely to appreciate God's wisdom, will find the greatest joy: *"A man's wisdom makes his face shine, and the boldness of his face is changed (8:1)."*

Once a person is out of the picture, there's no control over his possessions. This uncertain fate of all the fruits of his labor plagues him.[33]

כִּי־יֵשׁ אָדָם שֶׁעֲמָלוֹ בְּחָכְמָה וּבְדַעַת וּבְכִשְׁרוֹן וּלְאָדָם שֶׁלֹּא עָמַל־בּוֹ יִתְּנֶנּוּ חֶלְקוֹ גַּם־זֶה הֶבֶל וְרָעָה רַבָּה

"For there is a man whose labor is with wisdom, and with knowledge, and with skill; yet to a man that has not labored in it shall he leave it for his portion. This also is vanity and a great evil (2:21)."

Koheles already said above that he disliked leaving his work to someone else. So what is he adding here?

He is adding the idea that on one hand, accomplishment offers some recompense for all one's toil. But if someone else obtains more than you without working, your feeling of accomplishment is vanquished. The sense of accomplishment is a rationalization for all the work you went through to get where you are. But when another person attains more than you without effort, your labors lose their value. For wealth ends up in the lap of others at times without labor, like inheritances.

---

33) But this worry too, is futile. For the person concerns himself about an unknown matter, *"Who knows..."* Additionally, he is not alive when his possessions transfer to another. King Solomon expresses what he felt, but discounts it as futile, since in fact it does not diminish from the good life. It is a mere fantasy, and fantasies must not plague a person. Reality alone must be man's concern.

כִּי כָל־יָמָיו מַכְאֹבִים וָכַעַס עִנְיָנוֹ גַּם־בַּלַּיְלָה
לֹא־שָׁכַב לִבּוֹ גַּם־זֶה הֶבֶל הוּא

"For all his days are sorrows, and his labor grief; even in the night his heart does not rest. This also is vanity (2:23)."

King Solomon says he is in a state of constant pain. This exists whenever man strives for something. For all the while one strives, he is not yet where he wants to be. His inner desires aren't being met within reality.[34]

---

34) Anguish is yet another frustration associated with ambition.

ENJOYMENT

אֵין־טוֹב בָּאָדָם שֶׁיֹּאכַל וְשָׁתָה וְהֶרְאָה אֶת־
נַפְשׁוֹ טוֹב בַּעֲמָלוֹ גַּם־זֹה רָאִיתִי אָנִי כִּי מִיַּד
הָאֱלֹהִים הִיא

"There is nothing better for a man, than that he should eat and drink, and that he should make his soul enjoy good in his labor. This also I saw, that it was from the hand of God (2:24)."

The only good is eating and drinking.[35] What does he mean by *"it was from the hand of God?"* Verse 3:13 seems identical:

---

35) This is a real enjoyment and not a fantasy.

"And also that it is the gift of God[36] that every man should eat and drink, and enjoy the good of all his labor."

Verse 2:24 is a compound statement. The first part is supported by the next verse 2:25: *"For who can eat, or who can enjoy pleasure more than I?"* King Solomon means, that which is enjoyable, is the physical reality (2:24). Why is this what man enjoys? The answer is verse 2:25, i.e., because who else will?[37]

כִּי לְאָדָם שֶׁטּוֹב לְפָנָיו נָתַן חָכְמָה וְדַעַת וְשִׂמְחָה וְלַחוֹטֶא נָתַן עִנְיָן לֶאֱסוֹף וְלִכְנוֹס לָתֵת לְטוֹב לִפְנֵי הָאֱלֹהִים גַּם־זֶה הֶבֶל וּרְעוּת רוּחַ

"For God gives to a man who is good in his sight; wisdom, and knowledge, and joy; but to the sinner he gives the task of gathering and heaping up, that he may give it to one who is good before God. This also is vanity and a stressful spirit (2:26)."

Even though the king says to enjoy what you do; it depends on your psychological makeup whether you'll enjoy it or not. This is because there are two personalities [who cannot enjoy]: one personality is to consume, another is to accumulate. Since

---

36) If man looks into himself seeking accomplishment or other fantasies as the object of his drive for pleasure, he will find frustration. This is because fantasies cannot be satisfied by reality. Man invents impossible goals. But if man views his food outside the self, as a "gift from God," then he has separated his fantasies from the real food. Now he can enjoy the food, as he is not viewing it as a means to fulfill a fantasy, but simply as food. And food, isolated from a fantasy, can satisfy man. For now, man is functioning in reality; he is not seeking anything more than the food can offer, i.e., satiation and taste.

37) If man limits the expected satisfaction to himself, meaning not a fantasy, he can attain satisfaction.

the first type of person doesn't have the drive to accumulate; he possesses nothing to enjoy. And one who is driven to accumulate cannot stop and enjoy what he possesses, for his drive won't allow him to suspend his accumulation activities long enough to enjoy life.

Verse 2:26 comes as an answer to the last part of verse 2:24 where he says that everything is from God. Meaning, even though he said that you should enjoy things, nonetheless, it depends on how you are structured. He is showing how his last possibility for happiness isn't so easy either. Man must function in line with his nature.

PERMANENCE & SECURITY

לַכֹּל זְמָן וְעֵת לְכָל־חֵפֶץ תַּחַת הַשָּׁמָיִם

עֵת לָלֶדֶת וְעֵת לָמוּת עֵת לָטַעַת וְעֵת לַעֲקוֹר

נָטוּעַ   עֵת לַהֲרוֹג וְעֵת לִרְפּוֹא עֵת לִפְרוֹץ

וְעֵת לִבְנוֹת   עֵת לִבְכּוֹת וְעֵת לִשְׂחוֹק עֵת

סְפוֹד וְעֵת רְקוֹד   עֵת לְהַשְׁלִיךְ אֲבָנִים וְעֵת

כְּנוֹס אֲבָנִים עֵת לַחֲבוֹק וְעֵת לִרְחֹק מֵחַבֵּק

עֵת לְבַקֵּשׁ וְעֵת לְאַבֵּד עֵת לִשְׁמוֹר וְעֵת

לְהַשְׁלִיךְ   עֵת לִקְרוֹעַ וְעֵת לִתְפּוֹר עֵת

לַחֲשׁוֹת וְעֵת לְדַבֵּר   עֵת לֶאֱהֹב וְעֵת לִשְׂנֹא

עֵת מִלְחָמָה וְעֵת שָׁלוֹם

"To every thing there is a season, and a time to every purpose under the heaven. A time to be born, and a time to die; a time to plant, and a time to pluck up that which is planted. A time to kill, and a time to heal; a time to break down, and a time to build up. A time to weep, and a time to laugh; a time to mourn, and a time to dance. A time to cast away stones, and a time to gather stones together; a time to embrace, and a time to refrain from embracing. A time to seek, and a time to lose; a time to keep, and a time to cast away. A time to rend, and a time to sew; a time to keep silence, and a time to speak. A time to love, and a time to hate; a time of war, and a time of peace (3:1-8)."

What does King Solomon mean by "there is a time for these things?" He means that people try to maintain an attitude permanently. He is describing a certain security people seek in their actions and in their feelings towards things.[38] Therefore, by showing that there is time for each thing, he means that there is a limit.[39] This is similar to the role model feeling. Man sees someone successful and desires that life. However, the error is that man locks this person into a split second when he enjoys complete success. He then projects this fantasy image onto eternity and desires it for himself.[40]

---

38) Man is naturally uncertain about the future. This makes him insecure and fearful. Feeling that matters will remain the same provides a sense of knowledge and security about the future. King Solomon exposes this insecurity by saying man should not follow this natural disposition. A time for all matters means each attitude has an appropriate time, and limit.
39) That is, now might be the time for peace, but not later, when war is required.
40) One does not look past the present moment. Had he done so, he would learn of the frustrations that his role model endured prior and subsequently, and he would not be so fast to desire his life. Two errors exist: 1) one imagines the role model never endured frustrations or failures, and 2) one projects a fantasy where such role model success can be attained forever.

אֶת־הַכֹּל עָשָׂה יָפֶה בְעִתּוֹ גַּם אֶת־הָעֹלָם נָתַן
בְּלִבָּם מִבְּלִי אֲשֶׁר לֹא־יִמְצָא הָאָדָם אֶת
הַמַּעֲשֶׂה אֲשֶׁר־עָשָׂה הָאֱלֹהִים מֵרֹאשׁ וְעַד־סוֹף

"He has made every thing beautiful in his time; also he has set the world in their heart, so that man cannot find out the work which God has made from the beginning to the end (3:11)."

King Solomon discusses immortality. When man views one attitude in an eternal framework,[41] this prevents him from looking at the whole picture *"from the beginning to the end."* Imagining an attitude is eternal, one blinds himself to the outcome. Thereby, he cannot see the pitfalls.

יָדַעְתִּי כִּי אֵין טוֹב בָּם כִּי אִם־לִשְׂמוֹחַ
וְלַעֲשׂוֹת טוֹב בְּחַיָּיו

"I know that there is nothing better for them, than to rejoice, and to do good in his life (3:12)."

King Solomon gives an answer: the only good is to do good actions.[42]

Again, immortality is the required backdrop for a fantasy.
41) As he does when fantasizing about the role model.
42) This reiterates the earlier fundamental: man's actions, and not the fantasies he creates, do offer satisfaction.

וְגַם כָּל־הָאָדָם שֶׁיֹּאכַל וְשָׁתָה וְרָאָה טוֹב בְּכָל־
עֲמָלוֹ מַתַּת אֱלֹהִים הִיא

"And also that it is the gift of God that every man should eat and drink, and enjoy the good of all his labor (3:13)."

Someone who can enjoy his eating and drinking has the enjoyment of *"a gift from God."* Meaning, he is removed from feeling the emotion of accomplishment and can enjoy the temporal pleasure of themselves. The Chacham (wise man) described here, is not enjoying things via his feeling of accomplishment. Rather, he looks at everything as *"a gift from God."* We mentioned this truth above.

CONTROL

יָדַעְתִּי כִּי כָּל־אֲשֶׁר יַעֲשֶׂה הָאֱלֹהִים הוּא יִהְיֶה
לְעוֹלָם עָלָיו אֵין לְהוֹסִיף וּמִמֶּנּוּ אֵין לִגְרֹעַ
וְהָאֱלֹהִים עָשָׂה שֶׁיִּרְאוּ מִלְּפָנָיו

*"I know that whatever God does, it shall be forever;
nothing can be added to it, nor any thing taken from
it; and God does it so that men should fear before him
(3:14)."*

God created a perfect universe. It is foolish to say, "If only it
was this way or that way." This person doesn't see the perfection
in creation. Now, if man were able to manipulate the world to

satisfy all of his wishes, he wouldn't feel anything was out of his control. He would not possess fear of God. So there is a benefit in seeing that there is an order outside of man's desired order. A fool wishes that particulars do or do not occur. He doesn't accept the reality of a system of the world. But if he would recognize the system of the universe, he would not wish for these personal matters.[43]

---

43) One who recognizes the harmony in the universe, in Torah, and in justice, is overcome by a deep admiration for the Creator. Thereby, his personal desires become small in his eyes as compared to the magnificent precision and design of Creation and Torah principles. He then loses focus on his personal life, and even understands and accepts times when he experiences difficulties. He will view such difficulties as a natural result of universal laws, or even his own errors. He will see that such hard times must be experienced by most people. As he admires the system God created, he fully accepts that due to this best system, there will occur conflicts and occasional disappointments. But this does not mar his admiration for the system, or God.

JUSTICE

מַה־שֶּׁהָיָה כְּבָר הוּא וַאֲשֶׁר לִהְיוֹת כְּבָר הָיָה
וְהָאֱלֹהִים יְבַקֵּשׁ אֶת־נִרְדָּף

"That which is, already has been; and that which is to be has already been; and God seeks out the oppressed (3:15)."

King Solomon is discussing a person's wish that the future will offer change. He tells us it does not. But why does he bring in the idea that God will search out the oppressed, to punish the oppressor?[44]

---

44) Rashi 3:15

121

God's investigation of injustice doesn't improve matters, for the oppressed will still be oppressed. This is due to the fact that since man has free will, God won't interfere to save the oppressed.[45] This poses serious questions to philosophy.

What Koheles is teaching is that there are 2 cases. In the first case, one has achieved his ambition and its satisfaction fades. Or, one has yet to achieve his ambition. But when he does, he will suffer the same fate as one who already achieved his ambition. Thus, he can learn from his experience and how they effect him.

But there is another fate of man. That is, when someone has been prevented from his achievement by others. What often happens is he fastens his mind to the idea that his enemy will ultimately suffer. He thus does not gain the knowledge and wiles away his time with fantasies of retribution. This too is a fate of man: the unresolved ambition due to its being prevented by an aggressive foe, and its resulting mental state.

---

45) Of course, as Maimonides teaches based on numerous Torah sources, a person on a higher level of perfection earns God's protection. The oppressor will sin in his attempts to hurt such an individual, but God will save him. Perfection refers to a person who has acquired Torah truths and lives by them, while also avoiding Torah prohibitions through his control over his emotions and instincts. The Torah refers twice to "tamim", meaning perfect and without blemish: "Perfect (tamim) shall you be with Hashem your God (Deut. 18:13)." "Walk before Me and be perfect (Gen. 17:1)." The former refers to rejecting idolatrous beliefs, and the latter is regarding God's command to Abraham to perform circumcision. Thus, man is "perfect with God" when he 1) rejects all imaginary beings (idolatry), and 2) subjugates his knowledge to God's knowledge. When man accepts God as the sole authority on truth, following God alone, rejecting beliefs in all external deities or forces, and he subjugates his own internal thinking to God, man is then "perfect."

וְעוֹד רָאִיתִי תַּחַת הַשָּׁמֶשׁ מְקוֹם הַמִּשְׁפָּט
שָׁמָּה הָרֶשַׁע וּמְקוֹם הַצֶּדֶק שָׁמָּה הָרָשַׁע

*"And moreover I saw under the sun that in the place of
judgment wickedness was there; and that in the place of
righteousness, iniquity was there (3:16)."*

Man's desire for justice is not for justice per se. His motivation comes from the same desire for fame and lusts. Man seeks justice[46] for the sake of receiving honor. And once he attains honor, his desire for justice falls the way.[47] Seeking out a public office is for self-aggrandizement. King Solomon teaches here that there is no place where human corruption is absent.

אָמַרְתִּי אֲנִי בְּלִבִּי אֶת־הַצַּדִּיק וְאֶת־הָרָשָׁע
יִשְׁפֹּט הָאֱלֹהִים כִּי־עֵת לְכָל־חֵפֶץ וְעַל כָּל
הַמַּעֲשֶׂה שָׁם

*"I said in my heart, God shall judge the righteous and
the wicked; for there is a time there for every purpose
and for every work (3:17)."*

While it's true that there is no place where corruption doesn't take place, nonetheless, God will judge both the righteous and the wicked.

---

46) I.e., positions of justice, like politicians, judges, etc. Positions that offer man fame and glory.
47) I.e., once he attains his position, he no longer needs his former platform as a justice defender. Now he can indulge fame and glory, with no attention to defending truth and justice.

אָמַרְתִּי אֲנִי בְּלִבִּי עַל־דִּבְרַת בְּנֵי הָאָדָם לְבָרָם
הָאֱלֹהִים וְלִרְאוֹת שְׁהֶם־בְּהֵמָה הֵמָּה לָהֶם
כִּי מִקְרֶה בְנֵי־הָאָדָם וּמִקְרֶה הַבְּהֵמָה וּמִקְרֶה
אֶחָד לָהֶם כְּמוֹת זֶה כֵּן מוֹת זֶה וְרוּחַ אֶחָד
לַכֹּל וּמוֹתַר הָאָדָם מִן־הַבְּהֵמָה אָיִן כִּי הַכֹּל
הָבֶל   הַכֹּל הוֹלֵךְ אֶל־מָקוֹם אֶחָד הַכֹּל הָיָה
מִן־הֶעָפָר וְהַכֹּל שָׁב אֶל־הֶעָפָר   מִי יוֹדֵעַ רוּחַ
בְּנֵי הָאָדָם הָעֹלָה הִיא לְמָעְלָה וְרוּחַ הַבְּהֵמָה
הַיֹּרֶדֶת הִיא לְמַטָּה לָאָרֶץ

"I said in my heart concerning the sons of men, that God is testing them, that they might see that they are but beasts. For that which befalls the sons of men befalls beasts; one thing befalls them both; as the one dies, so dies the other; They have all one breath; so that a man has no preeminence above a beast; for all is vanity. All go to one place; all are from the dust, and all turn to dust again. Who knows that the spirit of man goes upward, and the spirit of the beast goes downward to the earth? (3:18-21)."

Man feels that he's chosen by God. This creates a sense of superiority (man chose God, or God chose man). This is a religious emotion.

"...that they are but beasts." This means that everything which man does can be reduced to his animal instincts. King Solomon is emphasizing man's innermost thoughts.

וְרָאִיתִי כִּי אֵין טוֹב מֵאֲשֶׁר יִשְׂמַח הָאָדָם
בְּמַעֲשָׂיו כִּי־הוּא חֶלְקוֹ כִּי מִי יְבִיאֶנּוּ לִרְאוֹת
בְּמֶה שֶׁיִּהְיֶה אַחֲרָיו

*"So I saw that there is nothing better, than that a
man should rejoice in his work; for that is his portion;
for who can bring him to see what shall be after him
(3:22)?"*

King Solomon concludes that all one has are his temporal
enjoyments.[48]

---

48) As discussed above, man's fantasies cause him concern over events after his death. But
this is fantasy If man would live in reality alone, he could enjoy his work.

SOCIALITY

וְשַׁבְתִּי אֲנִי וָאֶרְאֶה אֶת־כָּל־הָעֲשֻׁקִים אֲשֶׁר
נַעֲשִׂים תַּחַת הַשָּׁמֶשׁ וְהִנֵּה | דִּמְעַת הָעֲשֻׁקִים
וְאֵין לָהֶם מְנַחֵם וּמִיַּד עֹשְׁקֵיהֶם כֹּחַ וְאֵין לָהֶם
מְנַחֵם   וְשַׁבֵּחַ אֲנִי אֶת־הַמֵּתִים שֶׁכְּבָר מֵתוּ
מִן־הַחַיִּים אֲשֶׁר הֵמָּה חַיִּים עֲדֶנָה
וְטוֹב מִשְּׁנֵיהֶם אֵת אֲשֶׁר־עֲדֶן לֹא הָיָה אֲשֶׁר
לֹא רָאָה אֶת־הַמַּעֲשֶׂה הָרָע אֲשֶׁר נַעֲשָׂה
תַּחַת הַשָּׁמֶשׁ

*"So I returned, and considered all the oppressions that
are done under the sun; and behold the tears of such as
were oppressed, and they had no comforter; and on the*

*side of their oppressors there was power; but they had
no comforter. So I praised the dead who are already
dead more than the living who are still alive. And better than both of them is he who has not yet been, who
has not seen the evil work that is done under the sun
(4:1-3)."*

"...already dead" means that man's unconscious forces include
a self-destructive component.[49] But conscious instinctual forces go against self-destruction. People want to stay alive based
on an emotion for living, and a fear of death.

These verses are a natural conclusion from King Solomon's
dilemma. Death, or never being born solve life's problems.

What does oppression (4:1) have to do with this section? Ibn
Ezra says that praising the dead is a follow-up on oppression.
He addresses how man cannot tolerate oppression from man
[man cries due to oppression]. But man can tolerate God's oppression. Verse 4:4 answers this conflict. Man desires to impress others. This is a competitive emotion, and he labors not
solely to fulfill himself.[50] This ties into the fantasy of immortality: being accepted by everyone, he feels that this will last.

---

49) "Already" perhaps indicating a leaning towards self-destruction, like one who is head-
ing in that direction.
50) Oppression is the condition when man is not accepted. Thus, man possesses a need for
acceptance.

וְרָאִיתִי אֲנִי אֶת־כָּל־עָמָל וְאֵת כָּל־כִּשְׁרוֹן
הַמַּעֲשֶׂה כִּי הִיא קִנְאַת־אִישׁ מֵרֵעֵהוּ גַּם־זֶה
הֶבֶל וּרְעוּת רוּחַ   הַכְּסִיל חֹבֵק אֶת־יָדָיו
וְאֹכֵל אֶת־בְּשָׂרוֹ

*"And I saw that all labor, and every skill in work come
from a man's envy of his neighbor. This also is vanity
and a stressful spirit. The fool folds his hands together
and eats his own flesh (4:4,5)."*

King Solomon first describes the emotion of jealousy.[51] The
alternative is that a man *"eats his own flesh."*[52] This second individual isn't motivated by jealousy and ends up not accomplishing anything. This attitude is a reaction to the first.[53] Man's nature is that he has too much energy which needs to be satisfied.
Seclusion and simplicity – "folding his hands" in abandonment
of labor – to an extreme, will not provide essential needs and
any satisfaction. Man ends up frustrated. Either one of these
dispositions are wrong. But the second one is worse.

טוֹב מְלֹא כַף נָחַת
מִמְּלֹא חָפְנַיִם עָמָל וּרְעוּת רוּחַ

*"Better is a handful with quietness, than both hands
full of labor and a stressful spirit (4:6)."*

---

51) This ego emotion of competition drives man's labors.
52) One not motivated by jealousy will not work, and will become impoverished, i.e., "eating his own flesh:" metaphorically speaking as he has nothing else to eat.
53) Meaning, his envy can lead to real work, or to folding his hands in resentment.

According to Ibn Ezra, these are the words of the fool[54] whose rejection of labor (quietness) results in only one handful of food [i.e., poverty].

וְשַׁבְתִּי אֲנִי וָאֶרְאֶה הֶבֶל תַּחַת הַשָּׁמֶשׁ

יֵשׁ אֶחָד וְאֵין שֵׁנִי גַּם בֵּן וָאָח אֵין־לוֹ וְאֵין קֵץ

לְכָל־עֲמָלוֹ גַּם־עֵינָיו [עֵינוֹ] לֹא־תִשְׂבַּע עֹשֶׁר

וּלְמִי | אֲנִי עָמֵל וּמְחַסֵּר אֶת־נַפְשִׁי מִטּוֹבָה גַּם־

זֶה הֶבֶל וְעִנְיַן רָע הוּא

"Then I returned, and I saw vanity under the sun. There is a man alone, without a companion; he neither has son nor brother; yet there is no end of all his labor; nor is his eye satisfied with riches. 'For whom do I labor, and bereave my soul of good?' This also is vanity, indeed it is an evil matter (4:7,8)."

"There is a man alone, without a companion." Some try to live as a loner. However, by being alone you cannot accomplish: *"there is no end of all his labor."* This verse rejects individualism. *"For whom do I labor?"* describes the emotion to benefit others, which here goes unfulfilled.

The reason for the redundancy of *"alone, without a companion"* is this: not only do people have the one emotion of being individualistic, but that emotion includes another emotion: to exclude others from one's life. The *"aloneness"* is for the pur-

---

54) The fool wants ease, he is lazy. He does not exert himself, so he has nothing.

pose of *"without a companion."*

Rashi explains this idea of two being better than one. This extends to learning, where two are better than one. This also extends to social relationships, marriage, etc.

וְאִם־יִתְקְפוֹ הָאֶחָד הַשְּׁנַיִם יַעַמְדוּ נֶגְדּוֹ
וְהַחוּט הַמְשֻׁלָּשׁ לֹא בִמְהֵרָה יִנָּתֵק

"And if one prevail against him, two shall withstand him; a threefold cord is not quickly broken (4:12)."

Why are three better than two? The dynamics of two people engaged in study are such, that there still exists an undercurrent of "my idea against his idea." It's me against him. But with three, one is not pitted up against another. It is not a personal one-on-one matter. In Torah study (Rashi) objectivity is mandatory, but is found less when only two people study.

ELITISM

טוֹב יֶלֶד מִסְכֵּן וְחָכָם מִמֶּלֶךְ זָקֵן וּכְסִיל אֲשֶׁר
לֹא־יָדַע לְהִזָּהֵר עוֹד   כִּי־מִבֵּית הָסוּרִים יָצָא
לִמְלֹךְ כִּי גַם בְּמַלְכוּתוֹ נוֹלַד רָשׁ   רָאִיתִי
אֶת־כָּל־הַחַיִּים הַמְהַלְּכִים תַּחַת הַשָּׁמֶשׁ עִם
הַיֶּלֶד הַשֵּׁנִי אֲשֶׁר יַעֲמֹד תַּחְתָּיו   אֵין־קֵץ
לְכָל־הָעָם לְכֹל אֲשֶׁר־הָיָה לִפְנֵיהֶם גַּם
הָאַחֲרוֹנִים לֹא יִשְׂמְחוּ־בוֹ כִּי־גַם־זֶה הֶבֶל
וְרַעְיוֹן רוּחַ

"Better is a poor and wise child[55] than an old and foolish
king, who no longer knows how to take care of himself.

---

55) Rashi learns this to be a reference to the Yetzer Hatove, the intellect. Ibn Ezra says this refers to a child because a child doesn't have the ego yet. He asks out of pure inquisitiveness.

For out of prison he comes to reign; for in his own king-
dom he was born poor. I saw all the living who walk
under the sun, with the second child that shall stand up
in his stead. There is no end of all the people, even of
all who have been before them; yet they who come after
shall not rejoice in him. This also is vanity and a stress-
ful spirit (4:13-16)."

"*Better is a poor and wise child than an old and foolish king*" refers to Joseph and Pharaoh. At first, the masses viewed Joseph
as a nobody. And even after Joseph established himself, people
didn't recognize him, other than for being in the public eye.
But Joseph was better off even while in jail because he had the
potential.[56] The reason people valued him was because once he
became successful, they saw his greatness. But this was due
only to his accidental feature of holding a high position.

When it says people walked with the child, it means they
still didn't recognize him. In 4:16, "*yet they who come after shall*
not rejoice in him," means that even when he becomes king, he
is not recognized due to his wisdom, but rather, due to his ce-
lebrity status.

This depicts the false idea of royalty or society's elite. This
phenomenon is nonsense. For who would think of giving honor
to a lad? When he gets older, society suddenly endows him
with great importance. Thus, the masses are in a contradiction.

---

56) An inherent and independent value, as opposed to the dependent value attributed by the
public due to his famed position.

If on the one hand the child has inherent royalty, even during youth the people should show him honor. But they don't. And if there is nothing given to him at youth, why honor him as an adult?

SPEECH

שְׁמֹר רַגְלֶיךָ [רַגְלְךָ] כַּאֲשֶׁר תֵּלֵךְ אֶל־בֵּית
הָאֱלֹהִים וְקָרוֹב לִשְׁמֹעַ מִתֵּת הַכְּסִילִים זָבַח
כִּי־אֵינָם יוֹדְעִים לַעֲשׂוֹת רָע   אַל־תְּבַהֵל
עַל־פִּיךָ וְלִבְּךָ אַל־יְמַהֵר לְהוֹצִיא דָבָר לִפְנֵי
הָאֱלֹהִים כִּי הָאֱלֹהִים בַּשָּׁמַיִם וְאַתָּה עַל־הָאָרֶץ
עַל־כֵּן יִהְיוּ דְבָרֶיךָ מְעַטִּים   כִּי בָּא הַחֲלוֹם
בְּרֹב עִנְיָן וְקוֹל כְּסִיל בְּרֹב דְּבָרִים   כַּאֲשֶׁר
תִּדֹּר נֶדֶר לֵאלֹהִים אַל־תְּאַחֵר לְשַׁלְּמוֹ כִּי אֵין
חֵפֶץ בַּכְּסִילִים אֵת אֲשֶׁר־תִּדֹּר שַׁלֵּם
טוֹב אֲשֶׁר לֹא־תִדֹּר מִשֶּׁתִּדּוֹר וְלֹא תְשַׁלֵּם
אַל־תִּתֵּן אֶת־פִּיךָ לַחֲטִיא אֶת־בְּשָׂרֶךָ וְאַל־

תֹּאמַר לִפְנֵי הַמַּלְאָךְ כִּי שְׁגָגָה הִיא לָמָּה יִקְצֹף
הָאֱלֹהִים עַל־קוֹלֶךָ וְחִבֵּל אֶת־מַעֲשֵׂה יָדֶיךָ
כִּי בְרֹב חֲלֹמוֹת וַהֲבָלִים וּדְבָרִים הַרְבֵּה כִּי אֶת־
הָאֱלֹהִים יְרָא

"Guard your foot when you go to the house of God; to get near to listen is better than to give the sacrifice of fools; for they consider not that they do evil. Be not rash with your mouth, and let not your heart be hasty to utter any thing before God; for God is in heaven, and you are on earth; therefore let your words be few. For a dream comes through a multitude of business; and a fool's voice is known by a multitude of words. When you vow a vow to God, defer not to pay it; for He has no pleasure in fools; pay what you have vowed. It is better that you should not vow, than that you should vow and not pay. Do not allow your mouth to cause your flesh to sin; and do not say before the angel, that it was an error; why should God be angry at your voice, and destroy the work of your hands? For in the multitude of dreams and many words there are also many vanities; but you, fear God (4:17-5:6)."

The difference between a fool and a Chacham (wise man) is that the fool intersperses his fantasies in his words...in his *"multitude of words."*

"...and you are on earth; therefore let your words be few." As man is physical in nature (on Earth), he is irrational to an extent. Therefore, man is advised to minimize his words so as not to speak too much irrational talk.

Why is a vow mentioned here? One might think that it is perhaps true, when one normally talks, he can say foolish things. But when making a vow, it's coming from a different part of his nature[57] and therefore he will be able to keep it. However, one is better off not making a vow, *"than that you should vow and not pay."* This means one must not overestimate his power of keeping a vow. Maybe you really cannot fulfill your words.

"Do not allow your mouth to cause your flesh to sin; and do not say, before the angel, that it was an error; why should God be angry at your voice, and destroy the work of your hands (5:5)?"
This verse deals with the natural result of living this way.

"For in the multitude of dreams and many words there are also many vanities; but you, fear God (5:67)." Amidst the fantasies of life, one should try to maintain himself on the right track.

---

57) One might think by making a vow, he endows himself with added capacity to keep his word, than without making the vow.

EVIL

אִם־עֹשֶׁק רָשׁ וְגֵזֶל מִשְׁפָּט וָצֶדֶק תִּרְאֶה
בַמְּדִינָה אַל־תִּתְמַהּ עַל־הַחֵפֶץ
כִּי גָבֹהַּ מֵעַל גָּבֹהַּ שֹׁמֵר וּגְבֹהִים עֲלֵיהֶם

*"If you see the oppression of the poor, and the violent
perverting of judgment and justice in a province, do
not be amazed by it; for higher than the higher watches;
and there are yet higher over them (5:7)."* [58]

The verse addresses[59] man's nature in reference to evils and

---

58) Sforno explains *"higher than higher"* refers to God who is higher than the city's judges.
"Higher over them" refers to matters higher than the justice deserved by the corrupt judges.
Meaning, although evil officers deserve punishment, other considerations like maintain-
ing a city's order may require God to delay punishing the officials. Rashi says *"higher than
higher"* refers to God's messengers or angels whom God deploys to carry out justice over the
city's corrupt officials. The lesson is, although we may not see the justice we desire to see,
when we feel it is warranted, God has a system in place (angels) that the officials cannot
escape, as the angels are higher. God also decides the timing.
59) This verse is a response to man's question on apparent injustices. Man must not assume
he possesses all knowledge as does God, so as to lodge a complaint against God's methods
of justice.

injustices. Man wishes reality to conform to his subjective feelings of justice. However, God's system of justice doesn't match man's feeling of how God should mete out justice. The phrase *"higher than high"* means that there are set laws and considerations – "above" man's understanding – determining how the *Hashgacha* (God's providence) relates to man.

RICH & POOR

וְיִתְרוֹן אֶרֶץ בַּכֹּל הִיא [הוּא] מֶלֶךְ לְשָׂדֶה נֶעֱבָד

"And over all things land is more vital; for even a king must work the field (5:8)."

No matter how much a person has risen, he must realize that he always remains dependent upon certain things.[60]

אֹהֵב כֶּסֶף לֹא־יִשְׂבַּע כֶּסֶף
וּמִי־אֹהֵב בֶּהָמוֹן לֹא תְבוּאָה גַּם־זֶה הָבֶל

"He who loves silver shall not be satisfied with silver; and he who loves the masses and not grain; this also is vanity (5:9)." [61]

---

60) This truth must reduce man's projection of greatness onto the elite, for even kings are dependent beings and must eat.
61) Ibn Ezra explains: *"one who loves masses"* as one who acquires many servants so as to have the people before him.

The reason why one cannot be satisfied with silver is because it is only a replacement for food. Food provides satiety, but silver cannot because it is removed from the real pleasure.

A psychologist once said that people cannot be happy with money (silver) because there is no instinct for money. This means that since there is no innate desire for money, there is no place in the psyche for satisfaction. In order to be happy or satisfied from something, there must be a loss or a need in the person for that thing. But man's base drives do not include the emotion for the accumulation of wealth.

Rashi equates the accumulation of knowledge to this same emotion.

בִּרְבוֹת הַטּוֹבָה רַבּוּ אוֹכְלֶיהָ וּמַה־כִּשְׁרוֹן
לִבְעָלֶיהָ כִּי אִם־רְאִית [רְאוּת] עֵינָיו

"When goods increase, they who eat them are increased;
and what good is there to its owners, saving the behold-
ing of them with their eyes (5:10)?"

The only thing a rich man derives from his riches is fame alone, i.e., appearances. He is better off to maintain anonymity [forgo the fame] and avoid the trouble of others seeking his wealth at all times.

מְתוּקָה שְׁנַת הָעֹבֵד אִם־מְעַט וְאִם־הַרְבֵּה
יֹאכֵל וְהַשָּׂבָע לֶעָשִׁיר אֵינֶנּוּ מַנִּיחַ לוֹ לִישׁוֹן

*"The sleep of a laboring man is sweet, whether he eats
little or much; but the abundance of the rich will not let
him sleep (5.:11)."*

Due to his preoccupation with his work, the rich man does
not enjoy the pleasure of a good night's sleep.[62]

כָּל־עֲמַל הָאָדָם לְפִיהוּ וְגַם־הַנֶּפֶשׁ לֹא תִמָּלֵא

*"All the labor of man is for his mouth, and yet the ap-
petite is not filled (6:7)."*

His mouth refers to the instincts. Thus, man labors to satisfy
his desires. But man's soul isn't satisfied.[63]

כִּי מַה־יּוֹתֵר לֶחָכָם מִן־הַכְּסִיל
מַה־לֶּעָנִי יוֹדֵעַ לַהֲלֹךְ נֶגֶד הַחַיִּים
טוֹב מַרְאֵה עֵינַיִם מֵהֲלָךְ־נָפֶשׁ גַּם־זֶה הֶבֶל
וּרְעוּת רוּחַ

*"For what advantage has the wise man over the fool?
What has the poor man who knows how to walk among*

---

62) Another breakdown of the desire for wealth is that the rich man cannot enjoy one of the
most basic pleasures. People desire wealth based on what their fantasies tell them they can
purchase, or the associated fame they might receive. King Solomon reveals a few primary
sacrifices a rich man makes, thereby advising the reader to question the chase for wealth.
63) This was explained above (1:7); *"All the rivers flow to the sea, but the sea is not full."*

the living? Better is the sight of the eyes than the wan-
dering of the desire; this also is vanity and a stressful
spirit (6:8,9)."

Why should the one in the *ani* framework go after the wrong
way of life? *Ani* is the insignificant person. But it shouldn't
bother him to live while society puts him down.

In verse 6:9, King Solomon means that people want to be
recognized by others, *"Better is the sight of the eyes."* This, a person seeks to a great degree. The futility here is that although
man recognizes truths, he prefers to follow actions that will
achieve the recognition of others.

טוֹב לָלֶכֶת אֶל־בֵּית־אֵבֶל מִלֶּכֶת אֶל־בֵּית
מִשְׁתֶּה בַּאֲשֶׁר הוּא סוֹף כָּל־הָאָדָם וְהַחַי יִתֵּן
אֶל־לִבּוֹ

"It is better to go to the house of mourning, than to go to
the house of feasting; for that is the end of all men; and
the living will lay it to his heart (7:2)."

The first thing needed for a person to be happy is to envision
his death as a reality, like any other reality. Man must realize
that all the fantasies of mankind are just that: fantasies.

THE PSYCHE & PERFECTION

טוֹב כַּעַס מִשְּׂחוֹק כִּי־בְרֹעַ פָּנִים יִיטַב לֵב

*"Anger is better than laughter; for by the sadness of the
countenance the heart is made better (7:3)."*

Ibn Ezra comments:

*"It is known that when man's instincts are strength-
ened, the intelligence becomes weak and has no power to
stand before it, for the body and all[64] instincts strength-*

---

64) Perhaps indicating Rabbi Chait's lesson that when one instinct is aroused, this in turn
arouses all other instincts to seek their respective satisfactions. Rabbi Chait proved this
point from the incident of the Gold Calf. Once the Jews engaged in the idolatrous emotion,
they also sought to satisfy their carnal desires, as the verse states, *"They arose to make merry
(Exod. 32:6)"* – interpreted as illicit sexual activities (Rashi). Here too, Ibn Ezra says when
the instincts are strengthened, *"the body and all instincts strengthen the instincts."*

*en the instincts. Therefore, one who indulges in eating
and drinking will never become wise. [But] when one
joins the intelligence with one's ego, one may succeed
over the instincts. Then, the eyes of the intelligence are
opened a small degree and one is enabled to understand
physical science. However he cannot [yet] understand
the higher areas of wisdom due to the power of the ego
which strives for power; and it is that ego which creates
anger. And after the intelligence reigns over the base
drives via the assistance of the ego, the intelligence requires to be immersed in wisdom, that it will strengthen
it, until the intelligence succeeds over the ego, and the
ego is now subjugated to the intelligence (7:3)."*

Ibn Ezra teaches, when joining forces, the ego and the intellect can control the instincts.[65] [The person will create an intelligent plan to manifest a respected self-image by refraining
from base instincts that would generate public disdain. In this
manner, he has gained control over the instincts.] But he must
then work to eliminate his egoistical goals for power. This is
achieved through immersion in wisdom.

The idea of *"anger being better than laughter"* means it is better
to be involved in the ego which "gives birth to anger", than to

65) Ruling over our instincts enables our pursuit of wisdom. This enables man to engage the
intellect without distraction of emotional lures. Rabbi Chait explained that when we control
our emotions to be equidistant from both poles (viz., not too miserly or too spendthrifty) the
self (the ego) has neutralized the pull of that emotional spectrum. This works in any emotional spectrum, such as not acting with too much courage or shyness, too much morbidity
or jokingly, or too hastily or passively. Maimonides teaches *(Hilchos Dayos, chap. I)* that
by going to the opposite extreme temporarily, each person has the ability to work with his
specific natural leanings to†neutralize the emotional pole weighing on him. A lazy person
should therefore engage in extreme acts of zealousness, until he arrives equidistant from
either pole. He is then free of the pull of both poles in any emotional spectrum, with neither
pole drawing him, enabling his intellect freedom to act in line with God's will.

be under the sway of the instincts, the emotions. Now, once the emotions are controlled by the ego-intellect combination, the ego must be conquered through immersion in wisdom.

Rashi (1:12) shows the progression of removing one's self from the feeling of power. He says King Solomon was king over the world, afterwards only over Israel, after that only over Jerusalem, and finally king over his staff alone. This *midrash* means King Solomon slowly removed himself from the emotion of power until he reigned only over his staff. But why only over his staff? He should really reach to the extreme saying he wasn't king at all, as this would show the total removal of the emotion. However, "staff" means he was finally king over himself. He made the decision to conquer his emotions.

The ruling part of man requires knowledge. As he gains wisdom, it grasps hold of him. Once he is overcome by the love of wisdom, he will abandon his power drive (ego), and he will care only for wisdom. Striving for power will lose all of its appeal.

Koheles' ego is the "self". That part which one views as the "me." And this self changes with man's perfection. As man moves toward wisdom, this affects the person.

We realize, metaphysics and psychology aren't separate. The psyche is affected by perfection of the soul.

INTELLIGENCE

Human intelligence is limited by sight. But even this isn't accurate because solid matter as we see it, is truly mostly space. The way we see is via light reflecting off of objects into our eyes.

What do the Rabbis mean by *"light was set aside for the righteous people in the Messianic Era?"* [66]

We stated, light is the means for perception. Thus, a new "light" will be a new form of perception which will be made available for people living the correct life, and they will be able to use it for the sake of perfection. The reason why it wasn't

---

66) Rashi, Gen. 1:4

given originally was because the wicked people would use this knowledge for their own schemes. We see this expressed by superpowers that harness present-day knowledge for harm. How much more harm would occur if more knowledge was made available?

The Rabbis are teaching us that our senses fall short of being able to perceive the physical world perfectly. Our minds can make use of more knowledge if we had it. But our physical composition doesn't allow us to perceive reality as it really is.

INDEPENDENCE

וּמוֹצֶא אֲנִי מַר מִמָּוֶת אֶת־הָאִשָּׁה אֲשֶׁר־הִיא
מְצוֹדִים וַחֲרָמִים לִבָּהּ אֲסוּרִים יָדֶיהָ
טוֹב לִפְנֵי הָאֱלֹהִים יִמָּלֵט מִמֶּנָּה
וְחוֹטֵא יִלָּכֶד בָּהּ

"And I find more bitter than death, the woman, whose heart is snares and nets, and her hands are fetters; whoever pleases God shall escape from her; but the sinner shall be caught by her (7:26)."

King Solomon wants to know the cause of human evil. The verse says that this evil is a woman. But what does he mean by woman? Rashi says woman refers to is an apostate. Ibn Ezra says it refers to love. He goes on to say that for a wise man, a *chocham*, death is better. The state of love is one where man's ego is placed upon a woman. His energies are directed toward his love object. His self-esteem comes from the love object. Death being better than love means that for a chacham, if everything he does depends on his mate, he is not secure about himself and cannot function. The Torah is against a love in which one of the mates is totally dependent upon the other. Therefore, King Solomon's lesson is that ego depletion is the worst state.

Advertising works with this same principle, viz., "You are worthless without this object."

רְאֵה זֶה מָצָאתִי אָמְרָה קֹהֶלֶת אַחַת לְאַחַת
לִמְצֹא חֶשְׁבּוֹן

"Behold, this have I found, said Koheles, counting one thing to another to find out the sum (7:27)."

In order to gain knowledge, *cheshbon*, one must put together information piece by piece. A truly free investigation is one in which the person is not seeking an anticipated conclusion. The person must be independent.

אֲשֶׁר עוֹד־בִּקְשָׁה נַפְשִׁי וְלֹא מָצָאתִי אָדָם אֶחָד
מֵאֶלֶף מָצָאתִי וְאִשָּׁה בְכָל־אֵלֶּה לֹא מָצָאתִי

*"Which yet my soul seeks, but I find not; one man
among a thousand have I found; but a woman among
all those have I not found (7:28)."*

What prevented King Solomon from finding a woman in a
thousand? The answer is like the verse says, *"and to your hus-
band shall you cleave."*[67] By nature, a woman is more dependent
and hence, she is more removed from knowledge. *"Nashim
daatios kallos; woman are light-headed"*[68] means that as a rule,
women are naturally more subject to emotions than man.

---

67) Gen. 3:16
68) Kiddushin 80b, Sabbath 33b

GOOD & EVIL

שׁוֹמֵר מִצְוָה לֹא יֵדַע דָּבָר רָע וְעֵת וּמִשְׁפָּט

יֵדַע לֵב חָכָם   כִּי לְכָל־חֵפֶץ יֵשׁ עֵת וּמִשְׁפָּט

כִּי־רָעַת הָאָדָם רַבָּה עָלָיו   כִּי־אֵינֶנּוּ יֹדֵעַ

מַה־שֶּׁיִּהְיֶה כִּי כַּאֲשֶׁר יִהְיֶה מִי יַגִּיד לוֹ

אֵין אָדָם שַׁלִּיט בָּרוּחַ לִכְלוֹא אֶת־הָרוּחַ וְאֵין

שִׁלְטוֹן בְּיוֹם הַמָּוֶת וְאֵין מִשְׁלַחַת בַּמִּלְחָמָה

וְלֹא־יְמַלֵּט רֶשַׁע אֶת־בְּעָלָיו   אֶת־כָּל־זֶה

רָאִיתִי וְנָתוֹן אֶת־לִבִּי לְכָל־מַעֲשֶׂה אֲשֶׁר נַעֲשָׂה

תַּחַת הַשֶּׁמֶשׁ עֵת אֲשֶׁר שָׁלַט הָאָדָם בְּאָדָם

לְרַע לוֹ   וּבְכֵן רָאִיתִי רְשָׁעִים קְבֻרִים וָבָאוּ

וּמִמְּקוֹם קָדוֹשׁ יְהַלֵּכוּ וְיִשְׁתַּכְּחוּ בָעִיר אֲשֶׁר
כֵּן־עָשׂוּ גַּם־זֶה הָבֶל   אֲשֶׁר אֵין־נַעֲשָׂה פִתְגָם
מַעֲשֵׂה הָרָעָה מְהֵרָה עַל־כֵּן מָלֵא לֵב בְּנֵי־
הָאָדָם בָּהֶם לַעֲשׂוֹת רָע

אֲשֶׁר חֹטֶא עֹשֶׂה רָע מְאַת וּמַאֲרִיךְ לוֹ כִּי
גַּם־יוֹדֵעַ אָנִי אֲשֶׁר יִהְיֶה־טּוֹב לְיִרְאֵי הָאֱלֹהִים
אֲשֶׁר יִירְאוּ מִלְּפָנָיו   וְטוֹב לֹא־יִהְיֶה לָרָשָׁע
וְלֹא־יַאֲרִיךְ יָמִים כַּצֵּל אֲשֶׁר אֵינֶנּוּ יָרֵא מִלִּפְנֵי
אֱלֹהִים   יֶשׁ־הֶבֶל אֲשֶׁר נַעֲשָׂה עַל־הָאָרֶץ
אֲשֶׁר | יֵשׁ צַדִּיקִים אֲשֶׁר מַגִּיעַ אֲלֵהֶם כְּמַעֲשֵׂה
הָרְשָׁעִים וְיֵשׁ רְשָׁעִים שֶׁמַּגִּיעַ אֲלֵהֶם כְּמַעֲשֵׂה
הַצַּדִּיקִים אָמַרְתִּי שֶׁגַם־זֶה הָבֶל   וְשִׁבַּחְתִּי
אֲנִי אֶת־הַשִּׂמְחָה אֲשֶׁר אֵין־טוֹב לָאָדָם תַּחַת
הַשֶּׁמֶשׁ כִּי אִם־לֶאֱכֹל וְלִשְׁתּוֹת וְלִשְׂמוֹחַ וְהוּא
יִלְוֶנּוּ בַעֲמָלוֹ יְמֵי חַיָּיו אֲשֶׁר־נָתַן־לוֹ הָאֱלֹהִים
תַּחַת הַשָּׁמֶשׁ   כַּאֲשֶׁר נָתַתִּי אֶת־לִבִּי לָדַעַת
חָכְמָה וְלִרְאוֹת אֶת־הָעִנְיָן אֲשֶׁר נַעֲשָׂה עַל־
הָאָרֶץ כִּי גַם בַּיּוֹם וּבַלַּיְלָה שֵׁנָה בְּעֵינָיו אֵינֶנּוּ
רֹאֶה   וְרָאִיתִי אֶת־כָּל־מַעֲשֵׂה הָאֱלֹהִים כִּי
לֹא יוּכַל הָאָדָם לִמְצוֹא אֶת־הַמַּעֲשֶׂה אֲשֶׁר
נַעֲשָׂה תַחַת־הַשֶּׁמֶשׁ בְּשֶׁל אֲשֶׁר יַעֲמֹל הָאָדָם
לְבַקֵּשׁ וְלֹא יִמְצָא וְגַם אִם־יֹאמַר הֶחָכָם לָדַעַת
לֹא יוּכַל לִמְצֹא

כִּי אֶת־כָּל־זֶה נָתַתִּי אֶל־לִבִּי וְלָבוּר אֶת־כָּל־
זֶה אֲשֶׁר הַצַּדִּיקִים וְהַחֲכָמִים וַעֲבָדֵיהֶם בְּיַד
הָאֱלֹהִים גַּם־אַהֲבָה גַם־שִׂנְאָה אֵין יוֹדֵעַ הָאָדָם
הַכֹּל לִפְנֵיהֶם   הַכֹּל כַּאֲשֶׁר לַכֹּל מִקְרֶה אֶחָד
לַצַּדִּיק וְלָרָשָׁע לַטּוֹב וְלַטָּהוֹר וְלַטָּמֵא וְלַזֹּבֵחַ
וְלַאֲשֶׁר אֵינֶנּוּ זֹבֵחַ כַּטּוֹב כַּחֹטֶא הַנִּשְׁבָּע כַּאֲשֶׁר
שְׁבוּעָה יָרֵא   זֶה | רָע בְּכֹל אֲשֶׁר־נַעֲשָׂה
תַּחַת הַשֶּׁמֶשׁ כִּי־מִקְרֶה אֶחָד לַכֹּל וְגַם לֵב
בְּנֵי־הָאָדָם מָלֵא־רָע וְהוֹלֵלוֹת בִּלְבָבָם בְּחַיֵּיהֶם
וְאַחֲרָיו אֶל־הַמֵּתִים   כִּי־מִי אֲשֶׁר יְבֻחַר
[יְחֻבַּר] אֶל כָּל־הַחַיִּים יֵשׁ בִּטָּחוֹן כִּי־לְכֶלֶב חַי
הוּא טוֹב מִן־הָאַרְיֵה הַמֵּת
כִּי הַחַיִּים יוֹדְעִים שֶׁיָּמֻתוּ וְהַמֵּתִים אֵינָם יוֹדְעִים
מְאוּמָה וְאֵין־עוֹד לָהֶם שָׂכָר כִּי נִשְׁכַּח זִכְרָם
גַּם אַהֲבָתָם גַּם־שִׂנְאָתָם גַּם־קִנְאָתָם כְּבָר
אָבָדָה וְחֵלֶק אֵין־לָהֶם עוֹד לְעוֹלָם בְּכֹל אֲשֶׁר־
נַעֲשָׂה תַּחַת הַשָּׁמֶשׁ   לֵךְ אֱכֹל בְּשִׂמְחָה
לַחְמֶךָ וּשֲׁתֵה בְלֶב־טוֹב יֵינֶךָ כִּי כְבָר רָצָה
הָאֱלֹהִים אֶת־מַעֲשֶׂיךָ   בְּכָל־עֵת יִהְיוּ בְגָדֶיךָ
לְבָנִים וְשֶׁמֶן עַל־רֹאשְׁךָ אַל־יֶחְסָר
רְאֵה חַיִּים עִם־אִשָּׁה אֲשֶׁר־אָהַבְתָּ כָּל־יְמֵי
חַיֵּי הֶבְלֶךָ אֲשֶׁר נָתַן־לְךָ תַּחַת הַשֶּׁמֶשׁ כֹּל יְמֵי
הֶבְלֶךָ כִּי הוּא חֶלְקְךָ בַּחַיִּים וּבַעֲמָלְךָ אֲשֶׁר־
אַתָּה עָמֵל תַּחַת הַשָּׁמֶשׁ   כֹּל אֲשֶׁר תִּמְצָא
יָדְךָ לַעֲשׂוֹת בְּכֹחֲךָ עֲשֵׂה כִּי אֵין מַעֲשֶׂה

וְחֶשְׁבּוֹן וְדַעַת וְחָכְמָה בִּשְׁאוֹל אֲשֶׁר אַתָּה הֹלֵךְ
שָׁמָּה   שַׁבְתִּי וְרָאֹה תַּחַת־הַשֶּׁמֶשׁ כִּי לֹא
לַקַּלִּים הַמֵּרוֹץ וְלֹא לַגִּבּוֹרִים הַמִּלְחָמָה וְגַם
לֹא לַחֲכָמִים לֶחֶם וְגַם לֹא לַנְּבֹנִים עֹשֶׁר וְגַם
לֹא לַיֹּדְעִים חֵן כִּי־עֵת וָפֶגַע יִקְרֶה אֶת־כֻּלָּם כִּי
גַם לֹא־יֵדַע הָאָדָם אֶת־עִתּוֹ כַּדָּגִים שֶׁנֶּאֱחָזִים
בִּמְצוֹדָה רָעָה וְכַצִּפֳּרִים הָאֲחֻזוֹת בַּפָּח כָּהֵם
יוּקָשִׁים בְּנֵי הָאָדָם לְעֵת רָעָה כְּשֶׁתִּפּוֹל עֲלֵיהֶם
פִּתְאֹם   גַּם־זֹה רָאִיתִי חָכְמָה תַּחַת הַשָּׁמֶשׁ
וּגְדוֹלָה הִיא אֵלָי

Chapter 8

5. "Whoever keeps the commandment shall feel no evil thing; and a wise man's heart discerns both time and judgment.

6. Because to every purpose there is time and judgment, though the misery of man is great upon him.

7. For he knows not that which shall be; for who can tell him when it shall be?

8. There is no man who has power over the wind to retain the wind; nor has he authority over the day of death; and there is no discharge in that war; nor shall wickedness deliver those who are given to it.

9. All this have I seen, and gave my heart to every work that is done under the sun; there is a time when one man rules over another to his own hurt.

10. And so I saw the wicked buried, who had come and gone from the holy place, and they were forgotten in the city where they had so done; this also is vanity.

11. Because sentence against an evil work is not executed speedily, the heart of the sons of men is fully set in them to do evil.

12. Though a sinner does evil one hundred times, and his days are prolonged, yet surely I know that it shall be well with those who fear God, who fear before him;

13. But it shall not be well with the wicked, nor shall he prolong his days, which are like a shadow; because he does not fear before God.

14. There is a vanity which is done upon the earth; that there are just men, to whom it happens according to the deeds of the wicked; again, there are wicked men, to whom it happens according to the deeds of the righteous; I said that this also is vanity.

15. And I commended mirth, because a man has no better thing under the sun, than to eat, and to drink, and to be merry; for this will go with him in his labor during the days of his life, which God gives him under the sun.

16. When I gave my heart to know wisdom, and to see the business that is done upon the earth; for neither by day nor by night one's eyes see sleep.

17. And I saw all the work of God, for a man cannot find out the work that is done under the sun; because though a man would labor to seek it out, yet he shall not find it; and also if a wise man claims to know it, yet shall he not be able to find it."

Chapter 9

1. "For all this I laid to my heart, and sought to clarify all this, that the righteous, and the wise, and their deeds, are in the hand of God; no man knows whether it is love or hatred; all is before them.

2. All things come alike to all; there is one event to the righteous, and to the wicked; to the good and to the pure, and to the impure; to him who sacrifices, and to him who does not sacrifice; as is the good man, so is the sinner; and he who swears as he who shuns an oath.

3. This is an evil among all things that are done under the sun, that there is one event to all; also the heart of the sons of men is full of evil, and madness is in their heart while they live, and after that they go to the dead.

4. For to him who is joined to all the living there is hope; for a living dog is better than a dead lion.

5. For the living know that they shall die; but the dead know nothing, nor do they have a reward any more; for the memory of them is forgotten.

6. Also their love, and their hatred, and their envy is now perished; nor have they any more a portion forever in any thing that is done under the sun.

7. Go your way, eat your bread with joy, and drink your wine with a merry heart; for God has already accepted your works.

8. Let your garments be always white; and let your head lack no oil.

9. Live joyfully with the wife whom you love all the days of the life of your vanity, which he has given you under the sun, all the days of your vanity; for that is your portion in life, and in your labor in which you labor under the sun.

10. Whatever your hand finds to do, do it with your strength; for there is no work, nor scheme, nor knowledge, nor wisdom, in the grave to which you are going.

11. I returned, and saw under the sun, that the race is not to the swift, nor the battle to the strong, nor yet bread to the wise, nor yet riches to men of understanding, nor yet favor to men of skill; but time and chance happens to them all.

12. For man also does not know his time; like the fishes that are taken in an evil net, and like the birds that are caught in the trap; so are the sons of men snared in an evil time, when it falls suddenly upon them.

13. This wisdom have I seen also under the sun, and it seemed great unto me (8:5-9:13)."

Evil, is an attitude to change reality to conform to one's emotions. Here King Solomon identifies the cause of evil.

8:12 contradicts 8:14. 8:12 reads, *"yet surely I know that it shall be well with those who fear God, who fear before him."* While in 8:14, we read, *"...there are just men, to whom it happens according to the deeds of the wicked; again, there are wicked men, to whom it happens according to the deeds of the righteous..."* Another question is based on *"Because to every purpose there is time and judgment (8:6)."* What does "time and judgment" have to do with doing the mitzvah (8:5)?

Ibn Ezra says on verse 8:6 that a wise man doesn't wage war against one who is enjoying a successful hour. This means that an individual has good intuition in certain matters and will be successful.[69] The Gemara says that one should go into business with one who is successful. But what is the idea that a wise man knows that there are times of success for people? This means that a wise man doesn't overestimate himself. He realizes that reality won't change for him. So he deals with the situation as it is. But he will make a move against someone who is oppressing him, when he slips up. He doesn't sit back and wait for God to step in (eventually He will in time). He waits for the slip-up, and then moves in.

---

69) Therefore, the wise man will not try to fight this reality.

"For he knows not that which shall be; for who can tell him when it shall be (8:7)?" The wicked man, the *rasha,* doesn't think. He desires, and acts. He doesn't evaluate the results ensuing from his actions. The wise man anticipates. Here the verse says that even when it happens, *"for who can tell him,"* he doesn't even know, and he won't see the tragedy even when it's right in front of him.[70] The reason for this is since he is functioning with his emotions, he has nothing with which to investigate his actions. His mind is disengaged.[71]

Verse **8:8** literally states that one has no power over his day of death. *"...there is a time when one man rules over another to his own hurt (8:9)"* is another manifestation of situations in which one must realize that he has no control over the situation.

On verse **8:10** Rashi comments, *"I saw wicked people who came from another place and they came into the Temple and took it over. And they went home and were praised in the city from which they came concerning that which they did in the Temple. The Rabbis say that you shouldn't read וְיִשְׁתַּכְּחוּ (and they were forgotten) rather read the word וְיִשְׁתַּבְּחוּ meaning they will be praised and finally forgotten."* Rashi means that the praise these evildoers received displayed that their home townspeople valued their

---

70) He won't know that the tragedy is a punishment from Hashem. He attributes it to some other variable.
71) And therefore, he is outside the framework in which answers can be found.

conquest of the Temple. Praise is given for that which is valued. So even though their actions were wicked, when there is
success, people identify it with justice and they offer praise.
This ties in with verse 8:12 concerning the idea that the evil
person does not anticipate his downfall. Here too, the people
of the hometown are convinced this is a good and they can't
see the fault in it. Furthermore, we see that people succumb to
the vulnerability of being drawn in to a faddish success. The
"now" of this event is quite alluring. Even today, when institu-
tions wish to attract support, they rave about their successes.

In reality a person should never be swayed by success. It
is no argument for their position. In truth, the success of any
idea, is external to the idea. Ideas should be argued on behalf
of their internal logic.

אֲשֶׁר אֵין־נַעֲשָׂה פִתְגָם מַעֲשֵׂה הָרָעָה מְהֵרָה
עַל־כֵּן מָלֵא לֵב בְּנֵי־הָאָדָם בָּהֶם לַעֲשׂוֹת רָע

*"Because the sentence against an evil work is not ex-
ecuted speedily, the heart of the sons of men is fully set
in them to do evil (8:11)."*

King Solomon now addresses the questions which make it so
difficult to accept Judaism. He deals with philosophical points,
as well as emotional ones, touching on the point of success
we just cited. That is, even if we dismiss the issue of "suc-

cess", and claim that the conquerors of the Temple were wrong, we are still disturbed by their lack of punishment. This verse questions why there is no speedy punishment: people wish to see swift justice for the wicked, but they do not witness it. (On the *Az Yashir,* Rashi says that through the destruction of the wicked, God's fame is increased.) The following verse poses the same complaint:

אֲשֶׁר חֹטֶא עֹשֶׂה רָע מְאַת וּמַאֲרִיךְ לוֹ
כִּי גַּם־יוֹדֵעַ אָנִי אֲשֶׁר יִהְיֶה־טּוֹב לְיִרְאֵי
הָאֱלֹהִים אֲשֶׁר יִירְאוּ מִלְּפָנָיו
וְטוֹב לֹא־יִהְיֶה לָרָשָׁע וְלֹא־יַאֲרִיךְ יָמִים כַּצֵּל
אֲשֶׁר אֵינֶנּוּ יָרֵא מִלִּפְנֵי אֱלֹהִים

"Though a sinner does evil one hundred times, and his days are prolonged, yet surely I know that it shall be well with those who fear God, who fear before him. But it shall not be well with the wicked, nor shall he prolong his days, which are like a shadow; because he does not fear before God (8:12,13)."

Many righteous people suffered more than some of the greatest perpetrators of evil. The next verse, 8:14, strengthens this question and formulates it:

יֵשׁ־הֶבֶל אֲשֶׁר נַעֲשָׂה עַל־הָאָרֶץ אֲשֶׁר | יֵשׁ
צַדִּיקִים אֲשֶׁר מַגִּיעַ אֲלֵהֶם כְּמַעֲשֵׂה הָרְשָׁעִים
וְיֵשׁ רְשָׁעִים שֶׁמַּגִּיעַ אֲלֵהֶם כְּמַעֲשֵׂה הַצַּדִּיקִים
אָמַרְתִּי שֶׁגַּם־זֶה הָבֶל

*"There is a vanity which is done upon the earth; that
there are just men, to whom it happens according to the
deeds of the wicked; again, there are wicked men, to
whom it happens according to the deeds of the righteous;
I said that this also is vanity (8:14)."*

Regarding this question of why there doesn't seem to be punishment for the wicked, Ibn Ezra says[72] that there is nothing
more powerful or more difficult to answer. Does Koheles offer
an answer? Koheles inter-disperses some information within
the verses:

שׁוֹמֵר מִצְוָה לֹא יֵדַע דָּבָר רָע
וְעֵת וּמִשְׁפָּט יֵדַע לֵב חָכָם

*"Whoever guards the commandment shall know no
evil thing; and a wise man's heart knows both time and
judgment (8:5)."*

This verse employs the word "guards." Why didn't King Solomon say *"performs"* or *"performs Shabbos"* instead of *"guards a
mitzvah"*? "Guarding" refers to one who does more than mere
performance: he values the activity. King Solomon then ques-

tions why righteous people fall and wicked people prosper, and that *"a wise man's heart knows both time and judgment"*, meaning that there is justice. He intersperses this. (Verses 8:6 and 8:12 also say that there is justice.)

The answer is that on the whole, we do see justice. Through our thousands of years of persecution, we were still able to study Torah. There was ample time in which the Torah was studied, no matter how much our enemies tried to deter us. The splitting of the Red Sea illustrates the wicked and the righteous receiving their just rewards. Stepping back and viewing history over time, we find justice. But you cannot find it in the particular. Ibn Ezra says[73] that King Solomon understood the principle, but regarding the evil which occurs, he could not understand:

וְרָאִיתִי אֶת־כָּל־מַעֲשֵׂה הָאֱלֹהִים כִּי לֹא יוּכַל
הָאָדָם לִמְצוֹא אֶת־הַמַּעֲשֶׂה אֲשֶׁר נַעֲשָׂה
תַחַת־הַשֶּׁמֶשׁ בְּשֶׁל אֲשֶׁר יַעֲמֹל הָאָדָם לְבַקֵּשׁ
וְלֹא יִמְצָא וְגַם אִם־יֹאמַר הֶחָכָם לָדַעַת
לֹא יוּכַל לִמְצֹא

"And I saw all the work of God, for a man cannot find out the work that is done under the sun; because though a man would labor to seek it out, yet he shall not find it; and also if a wise man claims to know it, yet shall he not be able to find it (8:17)."

73) 8:17

As King Solomon says man cannot find out the works of God, how can he say in verses 8:12,13 that he knows that there will be good for those who fear God, and punishment for the wicked?

When King Solomon says that he knows *"there will be good for those who fear God"*, he is defining "good" by the value system of those who fear God.[74] And that is the performance of the mitzvos for their own sake, without an ulterior objective. Thus, the righteous do in fact enjoy that good life, and the wicked do experience tumultuous lives which don't permit their souls any harmony. This is what King Solomon "knows." The reason why Ibn Ezra said earlier that this area presents the most powerful questions, is because the typical person asks this out of an emotional basis and its carries with it much weight.

When Moshe asked God *"...please show me Your glory"*,[75] he was asking on a theoretical plane. He wasn't insecure about his beliefs. He knew that according to his design, following the ideas was the best life. But he wanted to know the theoretics. In contrast, when a typical person asks how the wicked enjoy good lives, he asks out of desire to secure [his own] reward for living a righteous life. In other words, typical people ask the following: *"What kind of punishment will the wicked receive? I see him living to a ripe old age. So why should I live the life of Torah? I won't lose out on what I really desire!"* Such a person

74) And not what is typically viewed as the "good."
75) Exod. 33:18

desires the Torah only as a means for some anticipated reward which he fabricates in his fantasies. However, the person living the correct life doesn't seek reward. He is totally engrossed in his studies; he is completely satisfied and seeks nothing else.

King Solomon also states that universally, we witness the righteous people being successful. He mentions this, for he wished to demonstrate that there is the factor of God's endorsement of the good life. This provides support for following the Torah lifestyle.

However, the question of how evil can happen to good people still remains a question. But the intellectual person places this question in the right place: theory. This question doesn't affect him practically: he knows without a doubt that the life that he already leads is enjoyable, and is the best life. A question on theoretics won't shake his conviction, which is 100% logical.

OVERESTIMATING LIFE

כִּי־מִי אֲשֶׁר יְבְחַר [יְחֻבַּר] אֶל כָּל־הַחַיִּים יֵשׁ
בִּטָחוֹן כִּי־לְכֶלֶב חַי הוּא טוֹב מִן־הָאַרְיֵה הַמֵּת

*"For to him who is joined to all the living there is hope;
for a living dog is better than a dead lion (9:4)."*

Ibn Ezra says that these verses are the incorrect views of
mankind. In verse 9:5 we see how much importance is placed
upon life: *"...but the dead know nothing, nor do they have a reward any more..."* One who voices this opinion says in other
words, "the dead know nothing and are nothing; life is everything." Verse 9:6 has the same meaning, *"...nor have they any*

more a portion forever in any thing that is done under the sun."

Emotions convince man that reality is defined by the here and now. That emotion is the previously-identified sense of modernity. "If you are *'connected to life (9:4)'* then you have value. But a dead lion, what's he worth? He doesn't have the here and now!" foolish people think.

These verses echo the masses' incorrect view, i.e., the over-estimation of life. This view results in an abhorrence of death. The denial of death soothes one's fears. And in doing so, he bolsters his fantasy of immortality. This person doesn't view reality as the reality of the soul. But in actuality, the duration of earthly life is very brief as compared to that of the soul.

לֵךְ אֱכֹל בְּשִׂמְחָה לַחְמֶךָ וּשֲׁתֵה בְלֶב־טוֹב יֵינֶךָ
כִּי כְבָר רָצָה הָאֱלֹהִים אֶת־מַעֲשֶׂיךָ

"Go your way, eat your bread with joy, and drink your wine with a merry heart; for God has already accepted your works (9:7)."

Rashi says this refers to the righteous man living a good life. Ibn Ezra says that these words are the feelings of the masses, whom King Solomon is now condemning. If so, what then is meant by *"God has already accepted your works"*? A concern for God's approval doesn't sound like something the masses would say, concerning their own opinions.

In truth, the masses are speaking here. But what they mean is to live life without guilt. They can't tolerate the conflict. So they say, "Just be happy with what you're doing."[76]

The succeeding verses follow the same tenor. The end of verse 9:10 states this view again, *"...for there is no work, nor scheme, nor knowledge, nor wisdom, in the grave to which you are going."* Meaning, once you are dead, that's it. Therefore, the masses again conclude that earthly life alone is what you should value.

שַׁבְתִּי וְרָאֹה תַּחַת־הַשֶּׁמֶשׁ כִּי לֹא לַקַּלִּים
הַמֵּרוֹץ וְלֹא לַגִּבּוֹרִים הַמִּלְחָמָה וְגַם לֹא
לַחֲכָמִים לֶחֶם וְגַם לֹא לַנְּבֹנִים עֹשֶׁר וְגַם לֹא
לַיֹּדְעִים חֵן כִּי־עֵת וָפֶגַע יִקְרֶה אֶת־כֻּלָּם
כִּי גַּם לֹא־יֵדַע הָאָדָם אֶת־עִתּוֹ כַּדָּגִים
שֶׁנֶּאֱחָזִים בִּמְצוֹדָה רָעָה וְכַצִּפֳּרִים הָאֲחֻזוֹת
בַּפָּח כָּהֵם יוּקָשִׁים בְּנֵי הָאָדָם לְעֵת רָעָה
כְּשֶׁתִּפּוֹל עֲלֵיהֶם פִּתְאֹם

"I returned, and saw under the sun, that the race is not to the swift, nor the battle to the strong, nor yet bread to the wise, nor yet riches to men of understanding, nor yet favor to men of skill; but time and chance happens to them all. For man also does not know his time; like the fishes that are taken in an evil net, and like the birds that are caught in the trap; so are the sons of men

---

76) The masses say, *"God has already accepted your works"* as their justification for their chosen lifestyle of eating and drinking. They project onto God His approval of their lifestyle.

snared in an evil time, when it falls suddenly upon them (9:11,12)."

King Solomon now explains how the masses' previously-mentioned philosophy must fail. The "enjoy the now" life cannot provide happiness. The reason being, it is a fantasy: it includes only the good parts of life and conveniently omits that part of man's essence which brings ruin to his plans. All of his inner conflicts are left out, as is the case with all fantasies.[77]

---

77) Therefore, when reality strikes in the manner that unforeseen troubles occur, as they always do, and the fantasy of living this "enjoy the now" lifestyle is destroyed, man will grow unhappy.

THE WISE MAN

עִיר קְטַנָּה וַאֲנָשִׁים בָּהּ מְעָט וּבָא־אֵלֶיהָ מֶלֶךְ
גָּדוֹל וְסָבַב אֹתָהּ וּבָנָה עָלֶיהָ מְצוֹדִים
גְּדֹלִים   וּמָצָא בָהּ אִישׁ מִסְכֵּן חָכָם וּמִלַּט־
הוּא אֶת־הָעִיר בְּחָכְמָתוֹ וְאָדָם לֹא זָכַר אֶת־
הָאִישׁ הַמִּסְכֵּן הַהוּא   וְאָמַרְתִּי אָנִי טוֹבָה
חָכְמָה מִגְּבוּרָה וְחָכְמַת הַמִּסְכֵּן בְּזוּיָה וּדְבָרָיו
אֵינָם נִשְׁמָעִים   דִּבְרֵי חֲכָמִים בְּנַחַת
נִשְׁמָעִים מִזַּעֲקַת מוֹשֵׁל בַּכְּסִילִים
טוֹבָה חָכְמָה מִכְּלֵי קְרָב וְחוֹטֶא אֶחָד יְאַבֵּד
טוֹבָה הַרְבֵּה

"There was a little city, and few men in it; and there came a great king against it, and besieged it, and built great siege works against it; And a poor wise man was found in it, and he by his wisdom delivered the city; yet no man remembered that poor man. And said I, Wisdom is better than might; but the poor man's wisdom is despised, and his words are not heard. The words of wise men are heard in quiet more than the shouting of him who rules among fools. Wisdom is better than weapons of war; but one sin destroys much good (9:14-18)."

People value power over wisdom. Rarely do we find people engaging ideas and wisdom for the pure enjoyment, without any expectation. Verse 8:16 voices this: *"the poor man's wisdom is despised."* Only when the wise man puts his wisdom to practical use, do any others recognize him (viz., *"and he by his wisdom delivered the city."*)

The wise man is the one who abandons the values of the masses. He has no psychological need to obtain society's approval. He is unconcerned about the fame and successes of others, or their opinions about him. He pursues a life of wisdom because it is enjoyable, it is in line with his nature, and not for an ulterior motive.

זְבוּבֵי מָוֶת יַבְאִישׁ יַבִּיעַ שֶׁמֶן רוֹקֵחַ
יָקָר מֵחָכְמָה מִכָּבוֹד סִכְלוּת מְעָט

*"Dead flies putrefy the perfumer's oil; so does a little
folly outweigh wisdom and honor (10:1)."*

One sin outweighs much wisdom; more than wisdom and
honor is a little foolishness. This foolishness, Ibn Ezra says
refers to sin.

King Solomon lived perfectly, except for one sin, and this
caused the Torah to speak about him in a derogatory manner.[78]
However, we must ask why is it all or nothing? Why must those
in power function flawlessly, where even the smallest error ru-
ins him? The reason is that people create a perfect image of a
political figure. And this image can only be maintained in the
public's eye, provided the figure is consistent with the people's
view of him. Therefore, when he falters, the image is shattered,
even though the mistake might be a minor oversight.

King Solomon's oversight of his wives building idolatry was
described by the Rabbis as something which he performed
himself. Even though he didn't actually commit this sin, it was
attributed to him to show the severity of what occurred. The
severity could be like Koheles describes here, i.e., the marring
of a figure.

---

78) *"Then, Solomon built an altar for Kmosh, the disgrace of Moav on the mountain facing Jerusalem, and to Molech, the disgrace of Ammon (Kings I, 11:7)."* Although he did not build these
altars, the Rabbis said the altars were attributed to Solomon's construction, on account that
he did not dissuade his wives from building them (*ibid, Rashi*).

לֵב חָכָם לִימִינוֹ וְלֵב כְּסִיל לִשְׂמֹאלוֹ
וְגַם־בַּדֶּרֶךְ כְּשֶׁהַסָּכָל [כְּשֶׁסָּכָל] הֹלֵךְ לִבּוֹ חָסֵר
וְאָמַר לַכֹּל סָכָל הוּא

*"A wise man's heart inclines him to his right hand; but
a fool's heart to his left. And also, on the road, when a
fool walks by, his understanding fails him, and he says
to every one that he is a fool (10:2,3)."*

The heart of wise man "to his right" means that his emotions
are leaning toward success.[79] But this seems to contradict verse
10:4 that says a wise man can be overtaken by his feelings of
rulership. But the answer is that 8:4 is dealing with a wise man
who abandons his wisdom.

Additionally, the wise man's emotions aren't compulsive,
whereas the fool and the wicked man's emotions are. But if the
wise man leaves Torah, he too will become compulsive.

"...he says to every one that he is a fool" means that once foolishness overpowers the fool, it will be impossible to hide.[80]

---

79) Torah often identifies the correct path as the "right"path.
80) As if he was literally "telling" everyone he is a fool.

RULERSHIP

אִם־ר֣וּחַ הַמּוֹשֵׁל֮ תַּעֲלֶ֪ה עָ֫לֶ֥יךָ מְקוֹמְךָ֖ אַל־תַּנַּ֑ח
כִּ֥י מַרְפֵּ֗א יַנִּ֥יחַ חֲטָאִ֥ים גְּדוֹלִֽים

*"If the spirit of the ruler rises against you, leave not
your place; for deference pacifies great offenses (10:4)."*

If a person becomes wise, "he shouldn't leave his place." Ibn
Ezra says this means removing one's self from wisdom. For
once a man removes himself from learning, he must descend
back into the foolishness of the world.

Additionally, one who has acquired knowledge and leans towards rulership, if he abandons a life of wisdom, this desire for
power will take over and destroy him.

179

יֵשׁ רָעָה רָאִיתִי תַּחַת הַשָּׁמֶשׁ
כִּשְׁגָגָה שֶׁיֹּצָא מִלִּפְנֵי הַשַּׁלִּיט

"There is an evil which I have seen under the sun, as an error which proceeds from the ruler (10:5)."

Rulers err due to the emotion of a rulership. The Gemara states this is a very powerful emotion. The reason why he who leaves learning becomes foolish, is predicated on the fact that learning effects someone only while he's involved in it. But there is no permanent change made by learning for any protracted duration of time. The Gemara states, if one learns and then leaves learning, he will be ruined.[81]

---

81) A similar sentiment: *"Rav Shimon ben Lakish said, 'It is found [written] in Megillas Chassidim, 'If you abandon me one day, I will abandon you two days' (Tal. Berachos 68a)."* This metaphor is the personification of Torah; Torah is warning man. This means that when one leaves learning, the damage is greater than expected. Although man left his learning only one day, it will take two days to regain the level on which he was involved when he left it.

Learning is not simply a matter of opening the sefer (book) and studying. Man naturally falls back into his emotional framework all the time he is not engaging study. There is no neutral state: one is either involved in wisdom, or his emotions. Thus, to return to a state of mind of learning, man must first extricate himself from his emotional attachments, taking "one day", and then reengage his mind in thought, "a second day." And if one leaves learning permanently, as Rabbi Chait explains, he will be ruined. The damage is compounded.

FOOLS & LAZINESS

חֹפֵר גּוּמָץ בּוֹ יִפּוֹל וּפֹרֵץ גָּדֵר יִשְׁכֶנּוּ נָחָשׁ
מַסִּיעַ אֲבָנִים יֵעָצֵב בָּהֶם בּוֹקֵעַ עֵצִים יִסָּכֶן בָּם

"He who digs a pit shall fall into it; and whoever breaks a hedge, a serpent shall bite him. He who removes stones shall be hurt by them; and he who chops wood shall be endangered by them (10:8,9)."

Metzudas David says that Koheles doubles the cases in order to state that this is always the case. Why always? Since the activity is inherently irrational, man will never succeed in his endeavors.

181

עֲמַל הַכְּסִילִים תְּיַגְּעֶנּוּ אֲשֶׁר לֹא־יָדַע לָלֶכֶת
אֶל־עִיר

*"The labor of fools wearies him, for he does not know
how to go to the city (10:15)."*

The fool's emotions frustrate his desires; he can never
achieve his desire, *"go to the city."*

בַּעֲצַלְתַּיִם יִמַּךְ הַמְּקָרֶה
וּבְשִׁפְלוּת יָדַיִם יִדְלֹף הַבָּיִת

*"By slothfulness the beams collapse; and through idle-
ness of the hands the house leaks (10:18)."*

Why is laziness brought in here? Laziness is a feeling which
stems from the emotion that everything is going to be all right.
Laziness is a withdrawal from reality.[82]

A side note: the way for one to perfect himself must be accompanied by the knowledge that his childhood emotions are
false. He must be able to see this clearly.

---

82) And one who follows this feeling of laziness will not repair his home, or act to secure
other basic needs, and suffer the consequences stated.

DEATH

Why does King Solomon discuss death at the end of his book? The reason is because a correct philosophy of life must, by definition, incorporate the fact that life has a limit. All of the decisions one makes pertaining to his life must be based on the correct understanding of life. If one makes decisions thinking that he is going to live forever, his decisions will be erroneous.

This ends Rabbi Chait's lectures from 1986 and 1987.
A summary follows.

SUMMARY

Rabbi Chait teaches that King Solomon first validates him-self as worthy of teaching these fundamentals. To understand which life is best, Rabbi Chait stated that King Solomon then introduces us to man's psychological makeup. From man's great ambition to succeed, his surging energies, and his im-mortality fantasy, the king lays the groundwork – a map of the psyche – so we might appreciate his explorations into man's quest for happiness. Rabbi Chait highlights the central theme that man creates and chases fantasies, and that these are the "futilities of futilities." Man assumes there is something "addi-tional" in his pursuits. King Solomon exposes these fallacies.

On the surface, it appears that King Solomon contradicted himself in numerous verses. We learn this was not the case. Wisdom can be both a good and an evil, if we consider that these two views are voiced by two individuals: King Solomon praises wisdom, while the masses deride it since they value earthly life, since "wise men die just as fools die." As wisdom doesn't save them from death, they criticize wisdom. One error of deriding wisdom is based on another error of believing earthly life to be all there is. There is no contradiction.

"More wisdom creates anger, and wisdom is also praised." This is resolved, as each sentiment is voiced by two distinct individuals. The fool is frustrated when he learns his desires are empty, so he grows angry. But the wise man who lives a life pursuing wisdom, and is not chasing empty dreams, will not experience anger. He praises wisdom.

If one views "the good" as his physical existence, God's justice is questioned. Life does have its let downs. However, the true good God intends for man is that which affects our souls; our eternal element. A fool will complain when he doesn't obtain every desire, while the wise man understands the physical is not perfect as an end, nor does he seek it as his goal. Rather, he finds wisdom to afford man the greatest joy. The wise man also lives by general rules and is not angered by isolated cases of difficulty, as is the fool. These two perspectives result in a wise man who is happy, and a fool who complains at every little inconvenience.

Ibn Ezra cites many verses[83] as the words of the masses; they are not the views of King Solomon. This alone resolves many other contradictions.

Following these principles, other contradictions too will be resolved.

---

83) 3:19, 9:4, 9:7

20013558R00109

Printed in Poland
by Amazon Fulfillment
Poland Sp. z o.o., Wrocław